D1636910

NIGHTCLUB NIGHTS

ART, LEGEND, AND STYLE

1920-1960

SUSAN WAGGONER

RIZZOLI
NEW YORK

CONTENTS

First published in the United States of America in 2001 by
RIZZOLI INTERNATIONAL PUBLICATIONS, INC.
300 Park Avenue South
New York, NY 10010

ISBN: 0-8478-2331-8
LC: 00-104397

Distributed by St. Martin's Press

Printed and bound in Singapore

FROM BABYLON TO BROADWAY

From time immemorial, mankind has gathered in groups,

large and small, dismissed care and worry and enjoyed especially

prepared food of higher quality than ordinarily consumed

together with rare wines while being entertained by dancers,

musicians, singers, magicians and buffoons . . . . We of today can,

at very nominal cost, enjoy food, drink, and entertainment

for which the Greeks and Romans would gladly have

paid a king's ransom and given a thousand slaves as a bonus.

Their crude musicians, their primitive dancers, and their torch

lights did not compare with present-day restaurant revues.

—INTERNATIONAL NIGHT LIFE

Live from the Hanging Gardens of Babylon—the modern nightclub! That was the way New York's International Casino saw things in its magazine, *International Night Life*, in the thirties. Far from seeing the twentieth-century club as a pale descendant of its ancestors, the Casino looked down and found the original plan much improved upon. According to them, it was only a hop, a skip, and a jump from the Colosseum to the Copacabana.

Well, not exactly.

At the turn of the century, public amusement in America was still an earnest imitation of public amusement in Europe. For the well-to-do and middle classes there were expositions and exhibitions, crystal palaces, and rooftop gardens. For the lower classes, beer halls with sawdust floors and traveling carnivals sufficed. Being a puritanical country, there were no Folies-Bergère or Parisian dance halls in America, but there *was* a great deal of food. Public sex might have been frowned on but public gluttony wasn't, and big bar-restaurants like Delmonico's and Maxim's provided all the entertainment one could want.

Then came Prohibition, splitting American nightlife away from its European cousins and forcing it in a different direction. On the night of January 16, 1920, revelers from Boston to Los Angeles enjoyed the last legal liquor that would be served for more than a dozen years. In New York, where it was bitterly cold and windy, there were mock wakes and funereal balls; the waiters at Maxim's dressed as pallbearers. The wise knew booze would still be available in one form or another, but the even wiser knew that nothing would be quite the same.

The pallbearers had dressed correctly: the great eating and drinking palaces, including Maxim's, Delmonico's, Bustanoby's, and Murray's Hanging Gardens, soon closed for good.

To accommodate the disaster of going dry, club owners and managers came up with a series of dodges and diversions. The end result was a circus of distraction so booming and spectacular it almost seemed to have been invented by design. Soon people were coming from all over the world to see the new American invention, the nightclub.

Despite its European connections, the American nightclub is a unique species. Born of hard times, it owes its existence to a distinct sequence of events. The name itself, "nightclub," was invented to circumvent Prohibition law. In theory, a nightclub was a private social club whose members gathered to eat, talk, and imbibe soft drinks. In reality, knocking three times could get almost anyone in anywhere, and the drinks were almost always of the hard variety. Despite all evidence to the contrary, the fiction was clung to with zeal. To reinforce the idea of legitimacy, entertainers were brought in.

Of course, no one was fooled.

Throughout the twenties, club owners were faced with a dilemma: to get customers, they had to supply booze. To supply booze, they had to violate the law and deal with bootleggers whose

The night club had a curious and diverse appeal.
To some it was a sex-exciter. To others, frequenting a night club and throwing away
money was a form of exhibitionism. Then, too, a great many Americans,
New Yorkers included, always have had only the most vague
and elementary notions of what constitutes a good time.

—STANLEY WALKER, *THE NIGHT CLUB ERA*, 1933

whole business was to violate the law. Federal agents, perfectly well aware of this, regularly raided nightclubs. In addition to shutting down clubs for selling illegal liquor, agents padlocked them for presenting floor shows without a theatrical license.

The whole business took on the air of an increasingly chaotic, never-ending scavenger hunt. Any evening out might or might not end in jail. Any club that was in business one day might or might not be padlocked the next. Since the places already were violating the Volstead Act, owners decided to ignore curfew and capacity laws as well. They also decided it was unwise to invest too heavily in furnishings and decor. Clubs became the kind of rough-and-tumble establishments Prohibition had hoped to quash, sporting names like the Furnace, the Hyena,

the Jail, the Ha-Ha, Bamville, the Drool Inn, and Glady's Exclusive Club, where the humor was as blue as the bluest June night. There were a few classier places as well, including New York's Lido-Venice, which was run by a group of society ladies. Here well-turned-out bouncers barred the riffraff, and the walls were likely to have been freshly painted and papered. Ironically, the refined establishments didn't excite people nearly as much as the more feral places.

The rudimentary nightclub had been born and roared along with the twenties in spite of Prohibition. Everyone wanted to get into the act. Even the infamous Evelyn Nesbitt, whose husband, Harry Thaw, had murdered her lover, architect Stanford White, in 1906's "crime of the century," opened a club. No longer a lush, sixteen-year-old Gibson-girl prototype, Nesbitt had descended into frumpy middle age, and the only memorable night her club ever had was the evening when Thaw, by then her former husband, threw the dishes onto the floor when presented with the bill.

Not only did the clubs stay in business, but they were able to charge prices high enough to cover the expense of doing business outside the margins of the law. During the twenties, nightclubs opened and closed, moved uptown, downtown, and across town with the speed of bursting champagne bubbles. Buildings that had been stables and bars and townhouses only months before were quickly—though not always elegantly—converted. One young man recounted an occasion when, deeply inebriated, he had found himself in a club that seemed hauntingly familiar. Hoping to sober himself, he went into the washroom for a splash of cold water, only to find his sense of déjà vu growing. He eventually realized the club was the house in which he had grown up, and the washroom in which he was standing had been his nursery.

The merry roar was stilled on October 24, 1929, when the stock market fell even farther and faster than the worst skeptics had predicted. Money that was thought to be in existence vanished overnight. Worse, millions who had bought on the margin discovered they were more than broke, they were deeply in debt. The effect on nightlife was almost immediate: Before the Crash, New York boasted more than seventy thriving nightclubs. By early 1933, barely a handful remained. Once again, nightlife had to reinvent itself. And once again, it did.

DINNER!

By 1930 it was clear that October 24, 1929, was more than just a day of "a little distress selling," as the house of Morgan insisted. The Depression was rolling—but so was the nightclub. Nightlife's salvation, according to *Fortune* magazine, was the "recent success of what is commonly known as the big Broadway joint, the gaudy bargain offer of fifty hot babies and a five-course dinner for $1.50 and no cover charge at any time."

Just who came up with the concept of pairing cheap grub with a splashy revue is uncertain. Some claim Billy Rose deserves the credit. Others say a man named Jules Ansaldi was the first to expand the pleasures of the old-style cabaret restaurant by moving it into a large, noisy room and adding a chorus of leggy showgirls. The basics of the idea had been around for a while, evident in the rooftop gardens and after-theater restaurants of the teens and twenties. But the scale on which "food" and "show" were paired in the years after the crash was something altogether new.

The allure of a menu bursting with appetizers, entrees, sandwiches, and side dishes can hardly be appreciated by today's standards. The idea of a continuous feast kindled a desire all its own. To walk into a club and know that, fifty or a hundred yards away, chef and staff stood at the ready to prepare the dishes one had taken for granted before the Crash, was an experience to be savored. Just reading the menu—with its promise of bluepoint oysters and roast leg of lamb—made people feel

THE MADEMOISELLE'S ROOM

LOU WALTERS LATIN QUARTER

CHOICE CHINESE DISHES FROM EAST TO WEST

EGG ROLL
1.75

ROAST PORK
2.50

SPECIAL BARBECUED SPARE RIBS 2.75

CHICKEN with FRIED RICE 3.25

SHRIMP with FRIED RICE 3.75

CHICKEN CHOP SUEY with MUSHROOMS 4.50

SWEET and SOUR SHRIMPS 4.75

SUBGUM CHOW MEIN with ALMONDS 5.25

MOO GOO GAI PAN 4.75
(Sliced White Chicken, Snow Beans, Mushrooms, Chinese Cabbage)

SHRIMP CHOW MEIN with MUSHROOMS 5.00

CHICKEN CHOW MEIN with MUSHROOMS 4.75

CHINESE PEPPER STEAK 5.50
(With Mushrooms)

LOBSTER CANTONESE 5.75

LOBSTER CHOP SUEY 5.25
(With Mushrooms and Bamboo Shoots)

LOBSTER CHOW MEIN
(With Mushrooms and Bamboo Shoots)

SHRIMP CANTONESE
4.75

5.50

SEE AMERICAN MENU ON REVERSE SIDE

At El Chico there is also excellent Spanish food, considered by connoisseurs to be the best in town. Those who have become squeamish about nightclub food in these difficult days can assure themselves by visiting the chef, Antoine Joffre, in his lair and marvel at his spick-and-span kitchen.

—GOURMET, APRIL, 1944

happy. And to get it all for a reasonable price, with a spectacular show thrown in, gave people hope in a way that Herbert Hoover never did. Small clubs that had charged twenty dollars before 1929 were now replaced by hippodrome-sized clubs with a cover charge of a few dollars or none at all.

During the hungry years of the Depression, the quality of the food didn't matter. Quantity was what counted. Chinese food, inexpensive and filling, became a club staple, especially in middle America, where egg rolls were still considered wildly exotic. In 1939, when rookie crooner Dean Martin played a nightclub in Columbus, Ohio, he was paid fifty dollars a week and all the chop suey he could eat. Everyone else had to ante up fifty-five cents. Even New York's Cotton Club and the glitzy Copacabana served Chinese food. Performers often complained about the ubiquitous fare, but when the Sands Hotel became *the* showspot in Las Vegas in the sixties, performers who had complained about Chinese food for years developed a sudden nostalgia for it, so the Sands kept it on the menu.

With the booming economy of World War II, the hunger pangs of the Depression faded. Military personnel ate courtesy of Uncle Sam, and civilians found work plentiful and well paying enough to keep the cupboard full of whatever wasn't rationed. For the first time in years there were people who cared about the quality of the dinner that came with the show.

Of course, not everyone cared what was on the plate. Only a handful of clubs ever reached a level of haute—or even middle-brow—cuisine. They did a whopping business nevertheless, and any club with plenty of booze, a lively floor show, a decent dance band, and an excess of noise and spangle had a shot at success. In the end it was the show, not the dinner, that drew customers.

. . . AND A SHOW!

And just what kind of show did patrons get with their dinner? Floor shows varied with the club, and each manager tried to give his revue a distinct flavor. At places like El Chico one could see an all-Latin (or nearly all-Latin) program, with rumba and mambo dance teams and a gypsy singer. There were the ethnic revues—the all-Chinese clubs of the West Coast and the "sepia" or "brownskin" shows of the East Coast. But the big-name clubs, the Latin Quarters and Cocoanut Groves and Copacabanas of the era, put on shows so large and diverse even the critics were hard put to define them.

THE MADEMOISELLE'S ROOM

LOU WALTER'S LATIN QUARTER

The ALL AMERICAN Menu

Hors d'Oeuvres

Jumbo Shrimp Cocktail	1.75	Smoked Nova Scotia Salmon	2.25
Chopped Chicken Livers Maison	1.50	Marinated Herring, Sour Cream	1.00

Entrees

Minced Chicken A La King	4.25	Double Lamb Chops	6.50
Broiled Spring Chicken	4.50	Filet Mignon with Mushrooms	7.50

Eggs

Ham or Bacon and Eggs	3.25	Omelette with Chicken Livers	3.50
Scrambled Eggs with Nova Scotia Salmon			4.00

Sandwiches

Latin Quarter Club Sandwich	3.50
Chicken Sandwich	2.50
Steak Sandwich	6.00
Hot Turkey	3.75

PRIME SIRLOIN
STEAK THUMBITS
$6.00

Desserts

Fruit Compote	1.50
Parfait Fantaisie	1.00

Ice Cream
or Sherbet
.75

SEE
CHINESE MENU
ON
REVERSE
SIDE

The large-scale revue had its roots in vaudeville, where audiences became used to, and developed a craving for, a jolting mix of singers, dancers, comedians, and novelty acts. A club would produce one or more revues a year, each with a theme and musical numbers that were somehow, however loosely, connected to that theme. The girls of the chorus sang and danced to songs that were written for the revue and, in nearly all cases, were totally forgettable. At the Latin Quarter, where mild naughtiness was prized, a revue called "Maid in Paris" featured songs with titles such as "Plastered in Paris" and "I Lost My Cherie in Paree."

Woven in, around, and through these numbers were the featured acts. Dancers were always popular. In the early years of the club era, Fred Astaire and his sister, Adele, danced to Emil Coleman's orchestra at the Trocadero in New York, while Clifton Webb and Mary Hay performed dance parodies at nearby Ciro's. Then came the Latin craze, and almost every nightclub had one—and sometimes two—Latin dance teams. With names like Veloz and Yolanda, Dorita and Valero, or Ramon and Renita, they tangoed and flamencoed across the floor with thrilling precision and sensual fervor. For folks who couldn't afford a ticket to Havana, where the mambo was a national institution, this was the next best thing.

Of course, all this dancing demanded music. Bands and orchestras did double duty, backing up the acts and providing dancing for patrons between shows. This was the era of swing, and the bands and orchestras were almost invariably first rate. Paul Whiteman, Guy Lombardo, Emil Colemen, Eddy Duchin, Xavier Cugat, Vincent Lopez—all were fixtures at one club or another. Glen Gray and the Casa Loma orchestra held forth at the Rainbow Room. At the Cotton Club, patrons were regaled nightly with the loose genius Cab Calloway. In addition to the club's big band or orchestra, there was usually a second band on hand to relieve them, making sure the club never lapsed into even a single moment of silence.

One of the more unusual staples of nightclub entertainment was the fortune-teller. At the classier clubs they were billed as "mystics"; at lesser clubs they were a good deal gaudier. When Dean Martin and Jerry Lewis performed at Chicago's Rio Cabana after the war, they were preceded by a fake Chinese fortune-teller whose act included a female assistant and a flock of pigeons. So common were fortune-telling acts in nightclubs that Jimmy Durante incorporated the gag into his own act, going from table to table making humorous prognostications. Picking the skinniest man in sight, he would peer into the man's palm and tell him he would soon inherit his weight in gold—and then advise a quick course of weight-building tonic.

Throughout the better part of the nightclub era, Jimmy Durante was the most popular comedian on the circuit. He began in the early twenties at a place called the Club Pizzazz on the far west side of Manhattan. Despite its glamorous name, the Pizzazz was little more than a bare floor in a square room, a former barn located in the rough-and-tumble neighborhood of Hell's Kitchen. Durante filled the room night after night and soon was getting bookings in clubs where brawls didn't break out as frequently as at the Pizzazz. Showman Billy Rose considered Durante almost the funniest performer he had seen, placing second only to Rose's wife, Fanny Brice. Durante was one of the few performers to have a club named for him, the Club Durant. In his book, *The Night Club Era*, raconteur Stanley Walker described Durante's brand of humor as so marvelously "violent and insane that even years later it was difficult to

The place was so crowded with adoring fans they literally hung from the rafters. They applauded, whistled, cheered, and roared. Schnozzola wasn't allowed to leave the floor; good-naturedly, he granted encore after encore.

—ABLE GREEN, EDITOR OF *VARIETY*

understand." When Durante played the Copacabana for the first time in 1943, the fight for space was so intense that tables went to the highest bidder. The club took in over sixty thousand dollars in a single week, and Durante's two-week contract extended into a three-month run.

Durante became famous in an era when fame meant nearly constant motion. Because cross-country air travel was still expensive, most performers traveled by bus or train, stopping between coasts to play dozens of nightclubs across the country. Even when performers stayed put, their schedules were often grueling. There were at least two shows a day, and headliners didn't have the luxury of understudies. Third shows, common at the most popular clubs, didn't begin until two or three in the morning. At the Club 500 in Atlantic City, they started at four and ended at dawn.

Moonlighting was also common, even for headline acts. At the end of the twenties, when Durante was playing the Silver Slipper in New York, he was also performing on Broadway and

JIMMY DURANTE'S DAILY SCHEDULE

8 A.M.–3 P.M. Filming at Paramount studio on Long Island

4 P.M.–4:45 P.M. Matinee at the Palace Theater

8 P.M.–9:50 P.M. First show at the Silver Slipper

10 P.M.–10:50 P.M. Evening show at the Palace

11:15 P.M.–3:30 A.M. Second show at the Silver Slipper

making a movie. When he was playing in *Red, Hot and Blue!* with Bob Hope and Ethel Merman in Chicago, he'd leave after the final curtain and turn up at Chez Paree in time to do the late show.

Nightclub comedians were almost always men. However, there were a few exceptions. There was the witty, sophisticated Beatrice Lillie, who began in London and was one of the few foreign stars to regularly wow American audiences. Later, as nightclubs shrank into smaller cabarets, an unknown, Carol Burnett, stepped onto the stage of the Blue Angel and sang "I Made a Fool of Myself Over John Foster Dulles" so hilariously she became an instant success. Short though the list of comedic women was, there was one who rose almost as high as Durante on the fame circuit. Big, buxom Sophie Tucker was a vaudeville veteran before the nightclub was even born. Billing herself as "The Last of the Red Hot Mamas," she became the mistress of the teasing innuendo, famous for tunes like "The Older They Get the Younger They Want 'Em" and "You Can't Deep Freeze a Red Hot Mama." Immensely popular with crowds, she was able to command thirty-five hundred dollars a week during the Depression—a thousand dollars more than the famous female torch singers of the era. As a performer, she was nearly indestructible, surviving both vaudeville and the golden era of the club. Tucker became a frequent guest on television variety shows and in 1966 played the Latin Quarter just weeks before her death at age eighty-two.

Ever mindful that audiences had a fair number of young couples on dates and older couples celebrating anniversaries, floor shows also included romantic crooners and torch singers. Some merely were good singers whose notoriety would not survive the era, adequate voices that would never have a record contract or gain national attention. Others were first-rate stars who continued to play the clubs long after their fame was established. Singer Helen Morgan, brought to fame by Billy Rose, lifted the torch singer's craft to art and went on to operate several clubs of her own—Helen Morgan's 54th St. Club, Chez Morgan, House of Morgan, and Helen Morgan's Summer House, all regularly raided and all eventually shut down by Prohibition enforcers. Then there was the scandalous Libby Holman, whose accomplishments ranged from challenging race and gender stereotypes to popularizing the strapless evening gown. In the talent department, Holman's voice was strong and smoky, and she became one of the great torch singers of the twenties and thirties. At the height of her fame she married Zachary Smith Reynolds, the twenty-year-old heir to the tobacco fortune. Reynolds, eight years Holman's junior, died of a gunshot wound in 1932, less than a year into the marriage. The case became a tabloid sensation, and Holman was arrested and tried for murder. Though acquitted, Holman was never completely able to live down the scandal. When she withdrew from public life to raise her son her singing career began to fade, a decline hastened by her dislike of "mechanical" apparatus. She did not want to sing with a microphone and, after appearing on television only once, refused to do so ever again. When her son was killed in a hiking accident in the late forties, Holman established a foundation in his name and dedicated her energy and wealth to the civil rights movement, which she supported until her death in 1971.

At the Cotton Club, one could hear torch singers par excellence. Here Aida Ward introduced "I've Got the World on a String"; Ethel Waters made "Stormy Weather" an instant hit; and Adelaide Hall belted out "Ill Wind."

If female torch singers could attract large crowds, so could male crooners. Tony Bennett, Vic Damone, and Julius La Rosa were all big on the club scene. The most famous singer of the century, the Voice himself, sang in nightclubs throughout most of his career. In July of 1939, Frank Sinatra was appearing at a little place called the Rustic Cabin outside Alpine, New Jersey. Bandleader Harry James heard the broadcast on the radio, drove out to New Jersey to have a look, and hired the twenty-four-year-old on the spot. Sinatra went on to sing in clubs across America. As a solo headliner he was especially associated with the Copacabana in New York and, later, the Copa Room of the Sands Hotel in Las Vegas.

Another nightclub sensation started out as a crooner but reached the pinnacle by doing a song-and-patter act with a goofy kid from Newark, New Jersey. Before their bitter split, the team became the most popular and most highly paid act in nightclub history. Dean Martin came out of the club circuit in his native Ohio. His first New York gig was at the Riobamba, filling in for Frank Sinatra, who had discovered he could make better money elsewhere. Reviewers were initially underwhelmed—at least until Martin proved wildly popular with the crowds and was held over week after week.

Martin's future partner, Jerry Lewis, also struggled at

the start, performing humorous pantomimes to records that played well in the Borscht Belt but weren't an entrée to the more sophisticated clubs of the big cities. Martin and Lewis's paths crossed when they were booked into the same clubs, and in early 1946 they were both playing the Havana-Madrid in New York. Their acts were back-to-back, and the two began heckling each other and kibitzing from the audience, much to the crowd's delight. After their contracts ran out they went their separate ways but came together again in the summer of 1946, at the 500 Club in Atlantic City.

Atlantic City on the Jersey shore had long been a boomtown for clubs and nightspots. There was the huge Steel Pier, which burnt down regularly but was always rebuilt; the Copa Cabana, which spelled its name differently than the New York club but got all the same headliners; the Dorsey brothers' Casino Gardens; and the Club Harlem, which featured black singers and dancers but not, alas, a black audience. Through the forties, the most popular nightspot in town was the Club 500. Known as "the Fives" to insiders, the club had entertainment up front and illegal gambling in the back. When Martin and Lewis found themselves playing there in July of 1946, they picked up exactly where they'd left off. While Martin attempted to sing, Lewis whirled around him in a comic frenzy. Within two nights, huge crowds lined up to get in. Sophie Tucker came over from the Copa, where she was booked, and gave the act her seal of approval. When they returned to the Havana-Madrid in September, the whole second half of the show was given to Martin and Lewis.

No act in nightclub history enjoyed the sudden, soaring nationwide success that Martin and Lewis did, and few acts ever earned as much money. When the two were booked into a hotel, the streets were clogged for blocks with fans hoping for a glimpse or an autograph. When they played the Chez Paree in Chicago, they made over twenty-five hundred dollars a week at a time when the average per capita income was only fourteen hundred dollars a year. They broke all-time attendance records; even with extra seating, the club's

He's lacking in personality, looks ill-fitting in that dinner jacket and, at best, has just a fair voice that suggests it would have little resonance without the p.a. system.

—*VARIETY* ON DEAN MARTIN, SEPTEMBER, 1944

A vocalist with definitely big possibilities.

—*VARIETY* ON DEAN MARTIN, DECEMBER, 1944

manager had to turn away two hundred people each night. At New York's Copacabana, they started at twenty-five hundred dollars a week and were held over at twice that rate, with a suite at the Hotel Fourteen above the club thrown in. At Slapsie Maxie's in Hollywood, they got four thousand dollars a week, while the biggest stars of the era fought to get a table. Lewis later recounted that Jimmy Cagney, Fred Astaire, Loretta Young, Joan Crawford, Edward G. Robinson, June Allyson, Humphrey Bogart, Clark Gable, Jane Wyman, Gene Kelly, and Gary Cooper all had been involved in the fray. When they played the Beachcomber Club in Miami over Christmas and New Year's of 1948–49, their price soared to twelve thousand dol-

I always have to break a song over my back.

I just can't sing a song; it has to be part of

my marrow and bones and everything.

—LIBBY HOLMAN

lars a week. Nine months later they got fifteen thousand dollars a week at the Flamingo in Las Vegas. Two years earlier, Lewis had been a one-hundred-and-fifty-dollar-a-week comic and Martin a three-hundred-and-fifty-dollar-a-week singer. Their partnership lasted a decade, breaking up due to personal tensions and Martin's desire to resume his singing career as a solo act. Their final nightclub appearance together was at the Copacabana on July 25, 1956, ten years to the day after they had first become a team.

The departure of Martin and Lewis was a sign of the changing times. With the rise of television and the suburbs, the nightclub era began to wane. People discovered they could stay home with their children and watch a spectacular show for free, even if it was on a small black-and-white screen and had frequent commercial interruptions. The big Broadway joint that had once been a gaudy and alluring bargain increasingly began to seem simply gaudy. The dinner-and-a-show days were fading. But oh, the glow they left behind.

BRINGING OVER THERE OVER HERE

The French Casino

A funny thing happened after World War I. All over the country, people discovered that it really was hard to keep 'em down on the farm after they had seen Paree. Some who had gone over, like Hemingway, simply forgot to come back. Others, like Scott and Zelda, hurried over to join their expatriate brothers and sisters. And those whose schedules and responsibilities limited their playtime took *aller-retour* jaunts on the White Star and Cunard lines, whose ships clogged the Atlantic. No doubt about it, Paris was all the rage. It was only a matter of time until someone realized that if Paris sold well in Paris, it would sell even better everywhere else.

If, on a night in the thirties, you had a sudden craving for the City of Light but found yourself in New York, you could indulge your passion at the French Casino. You could do the same in Chicago, Miami, and London, where there were affiliated clubs.

The New York club was especially large and lavish. Just a few years earlier, it had been the Earl Carroll Theatre, a four-million-dollar cavern carved out of Broadway's nightlife district. When the theatre failed, the space was leased to a new group of investors, who converted it into what *Fortune* magazine described as "a vast scarlet and silver restaurant which, in terraced rows of tables, seats fifteen hundred people without any crowding."

Entering the club must have given the impression of being swept along on a bubble of champagne. The club was a monument to the Deco era, with few straight lines and no corners to speak of. The lounge and bar area seemed to float beneath a ceiling that sloped, tentlike, toward the edge of the room and was striated with concentric bands. At the end of the room, a flight of stairs invited patrons up to an arched alcove

FRENCH CASINO

25¢

decorated with sleek female statuary. Inside the showroom, balconies swooped and curved. Tables on the main floor receded in graceful curving tiers. A cascading scroll of seating jutted from each wall. The metal handrails of the stairways resembled a series of weeping willow branches. Each chevron-shaped chairback was monogrammed with the letters "FC," which might as well have stood for "fun club."

Naturally, the sumptuous seating mandated food; in this case the proprietors boasted of a "hotel quality" meal, back in the days when hotel quality stood for something. Though earlier and later clubs often slipped into the habit of dishing up mediocre fare, the French Casino seems to have lived up to its boast. Reviewers generally agreed that the food was top flight, if not particularly French. The menu of May 4, 1936, informs us that "Le Diner Continental" came with a choice of appetizers that included both oysters and salmon, a soup course, vegetables, potato, salad, and a dessert finale in which one chose either sweets or cheese served on toasted crackers. The most expensive entrée was Sirloin Steak Maitre d' Hotel at four dollars, but one could indulge in the same feast by choosing an entrée of veal steak, grilled sole, or capon Florentine for less than three dollars. The menu also pointed to the club's big moneymaker, liquor, featuring much in the way of "Les Choixs des Cocktails." If the evening was a special occasion, you could add a bottle of Veuve Clicquot for twelve dollars or Moet & Chandon for ten dollars.

With these considerable attractions, the French Casino may not have needed a floor show. But, of course, it had one. The show was largely imported from Paris, which made the flashes of nudity seem sophisticated rather than tawdry. Nearly naked American girls parading on a stage had the ring of desperation, but nude French girls—well, that was Art. There were no headline acts in the show, but that didn't seem to bother anyone; in fact, that may have been a plus. The show had no dialogue which, as a contemporary reviewer pointed out, meant patrons could see the show any number of times without hearing the same jokes repeated.

The Casino made up for the lack of big-name talent by staging tableaux that were elaborate and even exotic. A woman named Mademoiselle Adalet dressed as a harem girl and did a slinky dance that left each man convinced of his own Sultan-hood. A man named Feral

"Nothing has ever approached it."

Seventh Avenue at Fiftieth Street

Columbus 5-7070

—FRENCH CASINO PROGRAM

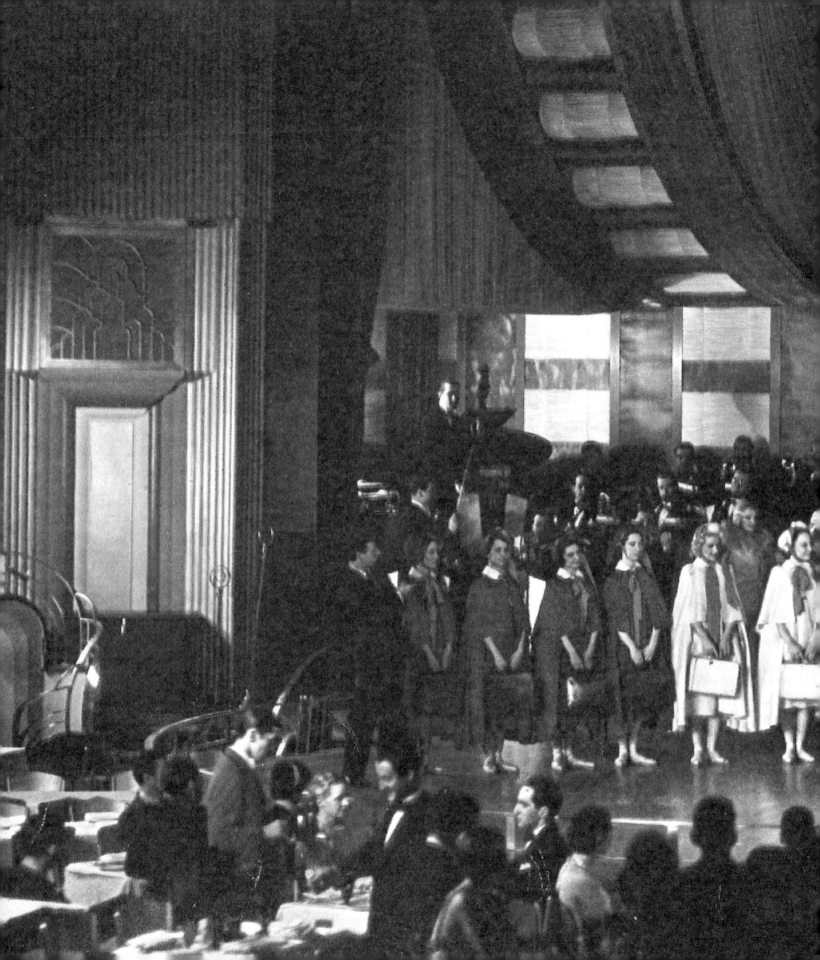

WERE CASINOS CASINOS?

Q: *WHICH OF THE FOLLOWING WERE ACTUAL CASINOS?*

A. THE FRENCH CASINO

B. THE LATIN CASINO

C. THE INTERNATIONAL CASINO

D. THE CASINO DE PAREE

The answer is none of the above. In America, where gambling was forbidden, there was tremendous appeal in suggesting the illegal and unavailable. Not one of these born-in-the-U.S.A. clubs had gambling. The French Casino clubs, with stateside posts in New York, Miami, and Chicago, featured imported French talent, while Philadelphia's Latin Casino and New York's International Casino built their revues around brand-name acts like Dean Martin and Jerry Lewis, Sophie Tucker, and Jimmy Durante. The Casino de Paree in New York and New Jersey's Casino Gardens reflected the straight-shooter reputations of their proprietors, Billy Rose and the Dorsey brothers respectively.

This isn't to say that gambling didn't exist. Backroom gambling was a staple for many clubs, almost all of which carefully avoided using the word "casino" in their names. Singer Dean Martin got his start at the Half Moon Nite Club in Steubenville, Ohio, his home town. He thought the showroom was elegant, until he saw the even plusher digs in the back, where the illegal casino was. In Atlantic City, New Jersey, the Dorsey brothers' Casino Gardens didn't have gambling but the innocuous sounding 500 Club did.

Even after World War II, when Las Vegas was created as a haven for gamblers, few establishments bothered to use the word "casino." The Flamingo, the Sands, the Desert Inn—all have the ring of sleepy little motels drowsing in the sun. Nevertheless, they were serious about their business. When Martin and Lewis played the Flamingo in 1949, Jerry Lewis ran up a one-hundred-and-thirty-seven-thousand-dollar gambling debt in a week. He asked club owner Bugsy Siegel why he had extended so much credit to someone he was paying only fifteen thousand dollars a week, but Siegel did not fall for the joke. It took Lewis a year and a half to repay the club in full.

Benga, clad in the briefest of briefs, thrilled the ladies with a number called "The Pearl Diver." For those in between or undecided, there was Renata Kramer, who dressed half as a man and half as a woman to seduce herself beside a painted lake. Beyond this there were production numbers, splashy and continental and triumphantly overproduced. The club's set designers were more imaginative than most, turning the Eiffel Tower on its side in one number and, in another, building eight-foot-tall busts of businessmen on top of which the girls posed provocatively. One season Johann Strauss, descendant of the composer, was brought over to conduct the orchestra. Another season featured Nina Chatalova and the Ballet Komarova as shopgirls of the Rue de la Paix. For those not in the know, the program patiently explained that "The Rue de la Paix of Paris is known as the avenue of all the smartest dressmakers and millinery creators."

After all this, patrons could make their way to the stage and dance—if they still had the energy.

The International Casino

Just five blocks from the French Casino was the International Casino, a club that billed itself as the "Eighth Wonder of the World," conveniently located in the heart of Times Square. The place was easy to find, even amidst the blinding lights of Broadway—it took two hundred and fifty feet to spell out the words "International Casino" in seven-foot-tall electric letters.

Once one passed through the solid brass doors and into the red and gold mosaic lobby, there was no shortage of amusements. The Cosmopolitan Salon was fitted with a small stage and littered with settees that could accommodate nearly eight hundred. Another one hundred and sixty could quench their thirst at the Spiral Bar, a curved slide of polished mahogany that swept from the ground floor up to the mezzanine. All this was a mere warm-up for the main room, where tiered platforms assured all fifteen hundred diners an unobstructed view of the show.

The Casino's owners were particulatly proud of their stage, a marvel of engineering driven by thirteen separate motors. No other nightclub had an orchestra whose reed section might suddenly plunge from sight, like riders on a parachute drop. Nor was all the fun reserved for the musicians. The stage itself also was equipped with "two disappearing stairways, every tread of which is automatically adjustable so that no matter in what position the stairways may be placed, every performer on them will stand at a ninety-degree angle. The stairways permit numbers in which the entire chorus descends through the ceiling." This was nothing compared to the two "mirror curtains" flanking the stage. Each weighed six thousand pounds and rode in and out of view on its own electric track.

Right at home in this Busby Berkeley–like setting was the show itself. Though the program stressed the club's international feel by describing "novelties from five continents and the beauties of ten countries," the show was indelibly American in its love of elaborate, large-scale fantasy. In the late thirties it hosted one of the most imaginative floor shows ever seen in a nightclub, the

Ice Frolics revue. Here, on a flooded stage, "Queen of the Ice" Evelyn Chandler performed midair somersaults and landed without a wobble. There was one fellow who skated on stilts, another who jumped a row of six large barrels, and a former world champion who performed a ventriloquist act with a Charlie McCarthy–like dummy. There were pretty girls too, of course—the members of the Skating Chorus did everything that other showgirls did, but at high velocity on narrow blades of tempered steel.

PALMS AND PIEROGI

Like an endless costume party, the nightclub era favored anything with a theme. The revues had themes. The menus had themes. Even the clubs themselves had themes. Exotic locales were always popular, and a single night in a single town could take you to Zanzibar, Versailles, Persia, Morocco, or Monte Carlo. Paris was the perennial favorite, both the high-toned Paris of the Folies-Bergère and the rougher, sweatier, sexier Paris of *apache* dancers and street musicians. There was the French Casino, the Casino de Paree, Chez Paree, La Vie Parisienne, and the Moulin Rouge—all of which were closer to Paris, Texas, than Paris, France.

Tropical settings were the most enduring of all, and a kind of palm frenzy gripped the era from start to finish. Early in the craze the flavor was Pacific, with cocoanut decor and seashell lamps and the occasional flamingo. There were numerous Cocoanut Groves, the oldest and most beautiful of which was located in the Ambassador Hotel in Los Angeles, and the most famous and tragic of which was located on the opposite side of the continent, in Boston. In New York's Hawaiian Room, Haleloke sang and did the hula, even on the coldest of January

nights. It wasn't long before the hula dancers and ukeleles were replaced by the rumba teams and conga drums, and tropical emphasis ran to things south of Key West. Clubs had names like Riobamba, Havana-Madrid, La Conga, El Chico's, and the Latin Quarter. New York's Copacabana, perhaps the splashiest and noisiest club ever conceived, was named for the well-known resort in Rio de Janeiro. There were endless variations of the name, from the Rio Cabana in Chicago to the Copa Room at the Sands Hotel in Las Vegas.

In addition to exotic locales, exotic cultures provided inspiration. Ethnic clubs like the Cotton Club and the Club Alabam' showcased African American talent even as they sought a whites-only patronage. On the West Coast, clubs like Kubla Khan's and the China Doll featured Chinese-born entertainers.

Of course, there were also clubs whose themes defied classification. Billy Rose's first nightclub, the Backstage, was rigged to resemble the backstage of a theater, complete with footlights, workings, and other bits of stage machinery. A place called Bimbo's in San Francisco was "home to the world-famed girl in the fish bowl." In Buffalo, New York, the Chez Ami featured a revolving bar that whisked patrons past the stage at regular intervals. The most imaginative of all may have been Kitty Davis's Airliner in Miami Beach, which billed itself as "the most unusual night

Even more exotic than *borsch* and Romanov exiles was the lure of Asia. One could find clubs from New York to Havana with names like the Tokio and the Golden Lotus, although the mix of singers, dancers, and showgirls was almost the same as it was at other clubs. The West Coast, with its rich mix of Pacific immigrants, was another story. Here, clubs like the China Doll, Forbidden City, and the

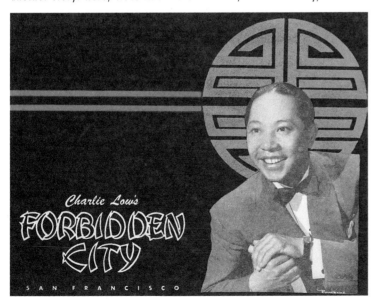

Dragon's Lair specialized in Asian revues that drew both Caucasian and Asian patrons.

Among the most famous of the Asian palaces was Kubla Khan's, which stood just beyond the enormous red-pillared gate of San Francisco's Chinatown. The club was operated by Eddie Pond, a multi-talented businessman who not only emceed the shows but danced in many of the numbers.

Kubla Khan's promised customers "a night in Chinatown"—a perfectly apt description since, like Chinatown, the show was neither Chinese nor American but a thrilling amalgam of both. At Kubla Khan's one could see the elegant dance team of Jadin and Li Sun as well as Noel Toy, a fan dancer in the tradition of Sally Rand. There were torch singers with flowers in their carefully rolled and chignoned hair and chorus girls dressed like harem girls. But there were also girls dressed in embroidered silk pajamas who could

balance a stack of teacups on each toe, and young men who carried on the tumbling traditions of the Chinese theater. Of course, there was a Latin band—Bill Oetke and his Rumberos, accompanied by Pond himself, who could play every percussion instrument from snares to castanets and who often billed himself as the "Chinese Demon of the Maraccos."

THE COCOANUT GROVE,
AMBASSADOR HOTEL, LOS ANGELES

club in the world." The club was an airplane, fitted with rows of banquette-style seating that faced a stage in the forward cabin. The plane took off, drinks were served, and the show began.

A clear contender for the "most intriguing award" in the theme-club derby had to go to La Maisonette Russe. The club, dreamed up by Prince Serge Oblensky, was meant to be a little bit of home for White Russians living out their days in New York exile. A priest from the Russian Orthodox Church sprinkled holy water over the club on opening night, and the club became an immediate success with those who favored an evening of refined Czarist entertainment. For homesick émigrés, the menu offered everything from *borsch russe* to *creme imperatrice* and *cafe turc.*

The *shashlik caucasien* was brought to the table by a brightly dressed Cossack who carried it aloft on a flaming sword. A young woman resembling an exceptionally well-dressed and perfectly made-up peasant brought tea from a steaming samovar. The showroom was not large, but it was saturated with enough old-world melodrama to start a revolution. The windows were wrapped with heavy, golden drapes and on the walls were murals of flying sleighs and troikas. The doorman wore a tight-fitting scarlet jacket festooned with buttons and braids. The orchestra was Slavic by way of Swing Street and could play everything from Tchaikovsky to "Tumbling Tumbleweeds." All in all, a night at La Maisonette Russe must have seemed like an intimate little evening on the banks of the Neva.

BILLY ROSE AND THE BIG NIGHT OUT

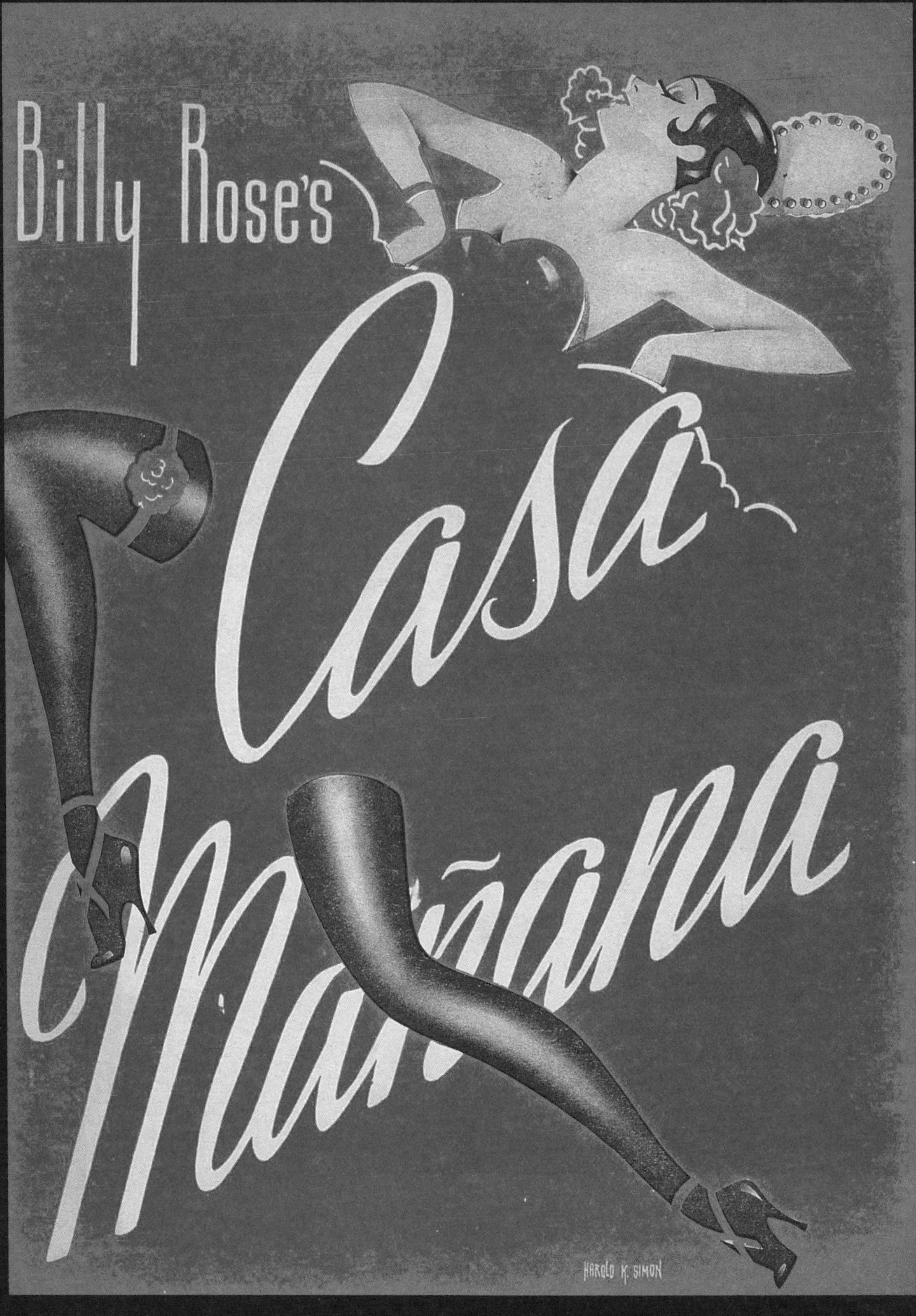

Billy Rose's
Casa Mañana
HAROLD K. SIMON

Born William Rosenberg in 1895, Billy Rose entered show business through a door in Tin Pan Alley and quickly proved himself master of the silly song with "Barney Google," a hit so lucrative it financed his first nightclub. In 1925 he opened the Backstage Club. Despite its location (over a garage in a less-than-chic neighborhood), the place was so crowded on opening night that Rose set up extra tables and asked the vocalist to sit on the piano. The club didn't last, but the new singer, Helen Morgan, did and made the piano perch her trademark. (Of course, like nearly everything in the nightclub world, there's an alternate version of this story: some claim that Morgan, whose lifelong problems with alcohol contributed to her early death, was simply too drunk to stand and was lifted onto the piano by Ring Lardner, who happened to be on hand that evening.)

Rose's problem with the Backstage was its popularity. Too many people came, demanding too much bootleg liquor, making it too lucrative for organized crime to ignore. In less than a year, Rose took his profits, bid farewell to his unwanted partners, and opened a classier (though equally short-lived) establishment in a better neighborhood.

Rose's clubs flourished despite Prohibition. Rose had a finely honed gift for knowing exactly what would make the public's pulse jump and was a firm believer in the Big Night Out. It was not enough for a club to be merely a club. It also had to have a theme, above-average food at below-average prices, liquor flowing like water, the illusion of sex, elephants, if possible—and, if the opportunity arose, a pool lapping the first tier of tables. He chose tall, leggy showgirls because he knew that long legs would kick higher and reveal a titillating flash of panties. At the Diamond Horseshoe, he dispensed with cover charges and kept the food prices low, giving the impression of an incredible bargain. Instead of making money on food, Rose placed full fifths of liquor on each table and let customers pour their own. Waiters were quick with ice and setups, and by the time the bill was totaled the account was settled in the club's favor. "No nightclub in history ever sold as much booze as I did at the Diamond Horseshoe," Rose once commented.

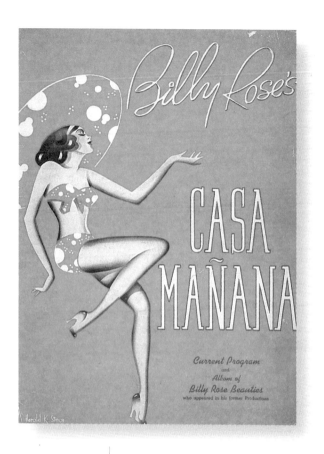

Though best known today as Mr. Fanny Brice, there was a time when Rose was one of the most recognized celebrities in America. He kept his Tin Pan Alley connection, collaborating on standards like, "It's Only a Paper Moon," "Me and My Shadow," and "I Found a Million Dollar Baby in a Five and Ten Cent Store." He produced Broadway shows, created large-scale extravaganzas, wrote a regular column, was heard daily on the radio, and was the key player in a number of nightclubs both in and outside New York. Anything he was involved with bore his name, usually in big, glittering letters. The water show that made stars of Eleanor Holm and Esther Williams wasn't just the Aquacade, it was *Billy Rose's Aquacade*. *Carmen Jones and Jumbo* weren't just Broadway musicals, they were *Billy Rose's Carmen Jones* and *Billy Rose's Jumbo*. When Life magazine proclaimed him "Public Showman No. 1," no one had to explain who Billy Rose was—Billy Rose was the Big Night Out personified.

The Casino de Paree

With the ongoing Depression, there were getting to be as many white elephants as white lights on Broadway. The owners of the New Yorker Theater offered Billy Rose one thousand dollars a week to take charge, providing him with the largest canvas and largest budget he had ever had at his disposal. Rose painted on a grand scale, creating the Casino de Paree by ripping out rows of seats and replacing them with tiers of tables and chairs that reached all the way up to the balcony. He brought in one of the city's best restaurateurs and asked him to conjure up a five-dollar meal, hired chorus girls who were employed for their ability to inspire goose bumps, and brought in headliners, including the new national sensation, Gypsy Rose Lee. The show was kept short to accommodate two seatings a night, but couples were invited to dance on the stage before and after the performance. The music, of course, was live—Benny Goodman and his orchestra—and from the moment the Casino de Paree opened in 1935, the place was a smash.

Casa Mañana

When Fort Worth, Texas, wanted something big for their 1936 centennial, they looked due east and hired Rose. It might have been a mistake—Rose, after all, was an easterner, born and raised on New York's Lower East Side; while he could produce the Big Spectacle, it wasn't yet known if he could produce the Big Texas Spectacle.

He could, of course, and the result was the Casa Mañana. It's a monument to Rose's sense of esprit that he donned cowboy gear instead of his customary business suit to be photographed, lariat in hand, astride a horse—a pose that could hardly have been comfortable or natural to him. He got his bandleader, Paul Whiteman, to do the same. To add local flavor, Rose auditioned Texas talent to augment acts brought in from New York. One local girl who didn't make the cut was Mary Martin. Rose felt she was too good for the chorus but not polished enough for a featured spot. "I am not running an amateur show," he told her, "come back when you make a name for yourself."

The whole undertaking was Texas–sized, with a chorus of six-foot-tall showgirls and enough hubbub to require two thousand costumes. In big-as-all-outdoors Texas, Rose was allowed to build his showplace from the ground up. The result was stupendous: a lavish amphitheater with seating for thousands

The whole stage moves
floatingly backward on its limpid
pool of real water and down into the lake
come real girls floating in real
boats. That's the finale.
What this has to do with the rest
of the show I never found out.

—ERNIE PYLE, *FORT WORTH PRESS*, JUNE 2,1936

and, at the focal point, the world's largest revolving stage. The complex stage could do more than revolve: as audiences discovered, it also could break apart to reveal a water-filled lagoon.

The consensus was that the show was tremendous fun. More than a million people came to see it during the centennial year; as a result, the show went into a second season. To keep the club's name in the news, Rose hit upon an ingenious publicity stunt. During the first year, he had noticed that many women didn't dance because their husbands or dates didn't ask them. So he brought in partners for them. The catch? Only bona fide British noblemen need apply. Those with pedigrees were offered a round-trip ticket from New York and seventy-five dollars a week. The plan was a success. Young men from the better classes considered the proposition a lark; the ladies were happy; their husbands and boyfriends were not the least bit jealous; and the most important customer, the press, made much of the stunt and kept the name of Rose and his club front and center throughout its second and final season.

For those who hadn't made the trip to Fort Worth, Rose opened a Casa Mañana in New York, taking over the space once occupied by the spectacular French Casino. In New York, there wasn't room for a seven-thousand-plus seating scheme or a stage that disassembled itself to accommodate a flotilla of gondolas. But there was room for the chorus of six-foot-tall showgirls, and Rose made up for the rest by filling the revue with big-name acts. For two dollars and fifty cents, which included a full-course meal, patrons could dance to Vincent Lopez and his orchestra and be entertained by Betty Hutton, Helen Morgan, and Abbott and Costello. Those who weren't interested in dinner could enjoy the show and dancing for just one dollar. Louis Prima and his orchestra also played New York's Casa Mañana, as did Jimmy Durante and Van Johnson, who made his debut there. The club opened in 1938 with a revue entitled "Let's Play Fair," described in the program as a gentle satirization of the New York World's Fair then under construction. Though it claimed to be "the only entertainment ever offered in a theatre-restaurant to have a book," it is uncertain whether or not the script was polished. What is clear is that, once again, the audience didn't care—the boisterous clamor, the food, and the fun were more than enough to satisfy.

The
Diamond Horseshoe

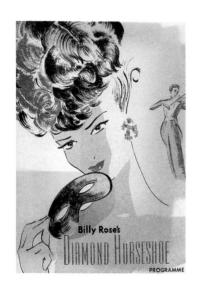

Billy Rose's
DIAMOND HORSESHOE
PROGRAMME

In the New York Casa Mañana revues, Billy Rose wanted to create a streamlined and updated kind of vaudeville. In his next club, he took a big step backward. The Diamond Horseshoe, located in the basement of the Paramount Theater, opened on Christmas of 1938. The cheerful songs of the day—"Jeepers Creepers," "Falling in Love with Love," and "You Must Have Been a Beautiful Baby"—belied reality. The Depression was far from over. In America, the unemployment rate was 19 percent and economic growth was still shrinking. In Europe, Hitler had just invaded Austria. Rose figured that what crowds wanted most of all was an escape to another time, an era altogether simpler, richer, and rosier in its outlook.

The Diamond Horseshoe was a nostalgic retreat that celebrated the vanished New York of Diamond Jim Brady and Lillian Russell. On the walls that led down the club's curving marble steps were murals depicting a gaslit New York, and early revues had titles like "The Turn of the Century," "The Silver Screen," and "Mrs. Astor's Pet Horse." Rose worked old vaudevillians into the revues, along with new discoveries like Virginia Mayo and a young and unknown choreographer named Gene Kelly. In 1943, Rose even managed to look forward by looking back, staging "The Post-War Preview" that paid homage to World War I while appealing to his customers' intense desire for the end of World War II.

The Diamond Horseshoe, the last of Rose's great clubs, had a long run. Clark Gable, Carole Lombard, Joan and Constance Bennett, Franchot Tone, Hedy Lamarr, and Noel Coward all patronized the Horseshoe, giving the club a stardust sparkle that kept the more common folk coming back. The club changed with the times, finding new ways to create bygone splendor, including a postwar review called "Violins Over Broadway." The show recreated the atmosphere of a European opera house and sported showgirls clad only in high heels and bikini–like outfits, each carrying a well-tuned violin and a long, graceful bow.

EARL CARROLL AND THE MODERN SHOWGIRL

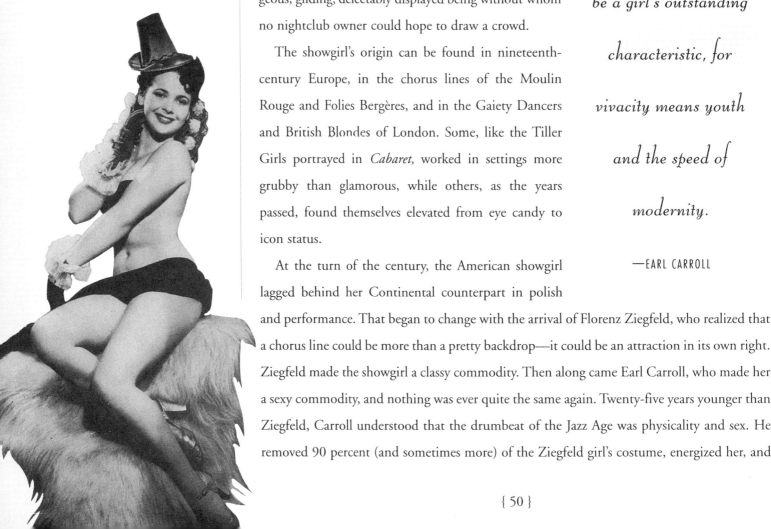

Ruby Keeler was one. So were Betty Grable, Lena Horne, Yvonne DeCarlo, and Sheree North. Mary Martin wanted to be one but didn't make the cut. Another one, named Barbara, became the fourth and final Mrs. Frank Sinatra. An earlier one, the frequently married Peggy Hopkins Joyce, was immortalized as Lorelei Lee in *Gentlemen Prefer Blondes* and played by Marilyn Monroe on the big screen. On the small screen, Lucy Ricardo wanted to be one but was toppled by her towering headdress. And on Broadway, *Guys and Dolls'* Miss Adelaide wanted to *stop* being one and *start* being Mrs. Nathan Detroit.

We're speaking, of course, of the showgirl, that gorgeous, gliding, delectably displayed being without whom no nightclub owner could hope to draw a crowd.

The showgirl's origin can be found in nineteenth-century Europe, in the chorus lines of the Moulin Rouge and Folies Bergères, and in the Gaiety Dancers and British Blondes of London. Some, like the Tiller Girls portrayed in *Cabaret,* worked in settings more grubby than glamorous, while others, as the years passed, found themselves elevated from eye candy to icon status.

At the turn of the century, the American showgirl lagged behind her Continental counterpart in polish and performance. That began to change with the arrival of Florenz Ziegfeld, who realized that a chorus line could be more than a pretty backdrop—it could be an attraction in its own right. Ziegfeld made the showgirl a classy commodity. Then along came Earl Carroll, who made her a sexy commodity, and nothing was ever quite the same again. Twenty-five years younger than Ziegfeld, Carroll understood that the drumbeat of the Jazz Age was physicality and sex. He removed 90 percent (and sometimes more) of the Ziegfeld girl's costume, energized her, and

The Ziegfeld clothes horse is passé. It's not enough for a girl to be beautiful and dumb.... Today, vivacity must be a girl's outstanding characteristic, for vivacity means youth and the speed of modernity.

—EARL CARROLL

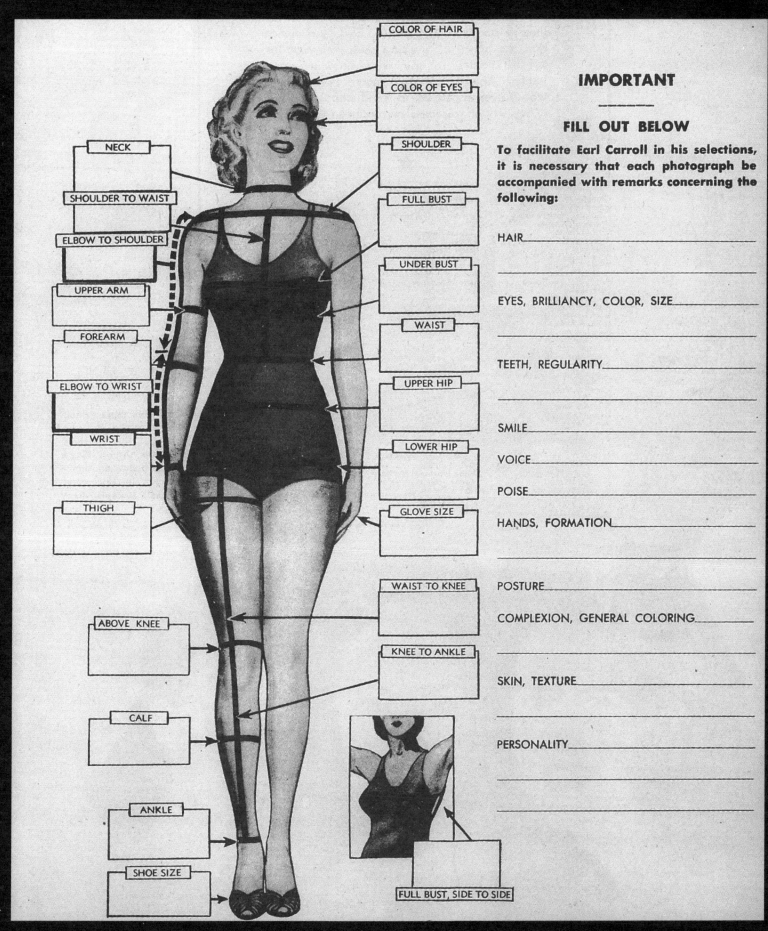

COLOR OF HAIR

COLOR OF EYES

NECK

SHOULDER

SHOULDER TO WAIST

FULL BUST

ELBOW TO SHOULDER

UNDER BUST

UPPER ARM

WAIST

FOREARM

UPPER HIP

ELBOW TO WRIST

LOWER HIP

WRIST

THIGH

GLOVE SIZE

WAIST TO KNEE

ABOVE KNEE

KNEE TO ANKLE

CALF

ANKLE

SHOE SIZE

FULL BUST, SIDE TO SIDE

IMPORTANT

FILL OUT BELOW

To facilitate Earl Carroll in his selections, it is necessary that each photograph be accompanied with remarks concerning the following:

HAIR _____

_____

EYES, BRILLIANCY, COLOR, SIZE _____

_____

TEETH, REGULARITY _____

_____

SMILE _____

VOICE _____

POISE _____

HANDS, FORMATION _____

_____

POSTURE _____

COMPLEXION, GENERAL COLORING _____

_____

SKIN, TEXTURE _____

_____

PERSONALITY _____

_____

_____

BEAUT

PARADE

EARL CARROLL'S TEN DEMANDMENTS OF BEAUTY

1. The most important is a double header. Don't under-value or over-value your beauty. Remember that the world is filled with thousands of beautiful women and the homage you receive from men and women is given to any lovely girl.

4. Don't marry too young. Great beauties usually become dissatisfied with an early marriage, feeling that they have missed great opportunities for a fuller life by assuming the duties of motherhood and wifehood before their time.

Don't over-value your gifts of nature to the extent of not developing a charming personality and a fine, alert mind. The stage never tolerates for long the combination called "beautiful and dumb." Furthermore, the life of a stage beauty is seldom longer than five years, so it behooves all lovely women to store something up for the years when the blooming is over.

There are a few women, especially in this country, who under-value their beauty. These women usually go to the opposite extreme of those who over-value pulchritude, in developing a mental life to the exclusion of their beauty. Even the greatest natural beauty in the world requires molding, finishing and retouching. No woman ever became world-famous for her beauty without training in poise, grace, clothes and even voice culture.

2. Don't permit the whirl of social life to rob you of youth before your time. So many times I have seen the tragedy of beautiful girls finding the lure of the night clubs and admiring escorts irresistible, with the usual result of becoming unfit for "Vanities" or any other big New York show after one season.

3. Don't diet strenuously but keep your figure and face attractive with exercise and sensible eating. Extreme weight is never tolerated on the stage, and when any girl starts putting on weight she is sent to a physician who prescribes a healthy diet and routine for her.

5. Don't drink or smoke. Beauty depends first upon excellent health, and dissipation is no aid to beauty.

6. Don't listen to flattery. Learn to accept compliments with grace and charm, but never take the patter of your admirers too seriously. A conceited beauty loses much of her loveliness in arrogance.

7. Don't go in for strenuous sports too intensely. Too much golf, tennis or swimming causes muscular development, which is disastrous to the feminine figure.

8. Don't worry constantly over losing youth and beauty. Learn to take the advancing years gracefully, and when middle age arrives, do not try to imitate an eighteen-year-old girl.

9. Don't try changing the color of your hair. Nature usually selects the right shade of hair for all of us. If hair becomes faded from the sun, rinses will suffice, but never dyes. Natural beauty is always the loveliest.

10. Don't use too much make-up. Much natural beauty in America lies buried beneath coats of powder, mascara and paint. A touch of make-up on the eyelids, a light coating of natural powder and a lipstick should suffice as gilding for any naturally beautiful girl.

made her the star of his stage revues. For several seasons, Carroll's "Vanities" revues were the talk of the town.

Then public taste suddenly changed. Audiences wanted something faster, sprightlier, and more modern. The lavish stage revue quickly became as passé as the Ziegfeld "clothes horse." Carroll seemed to have lost his touch. He became a laughing stock on Broadway, someone whose career obit was written, in print or biting conversation, almost daily. When the playwright George S. Kaufman asked Groucho Marx what he thought of the new season's show, Groucho replied, "I had rather not say. I saw it under bad conditions—the curtain was up." Carroll divested himself of his theater, moved to Los Angeles, and

I am sure I am going to love the show. We have our costumes.

They are glorious and I have five changes and they make me look wonderful.

There is one number—"Furs"—where I come out dripping in chinchilla.

—FROM THE DIARY OF PEGGY HOPKINS JOYCE

reinvented his dream on a scale grander than ever. Back in New York, others had worked his invention, the sexy showgirl, into another invention, the nightclub. In California, Carroll decided to do the same.

Earl Carroll's Hollywood Theatre Restaurant opened on December 26, 1938. It was a gala opening, even though Carroll flaunted the fact that his club would feature no headline acts, just girls, girls, and more girls. Among those rioting to get in were Franchot Tone, Errol Flynn, Marlene Dietrich, Delores Del Rio, Clark Gable and Carole Lombard, Edgar Bergen (sans Charlie McCarthy), Darryl Zanuck, and David O. Selznick.

The club, which bore the motto, "Through these portals pass the most beautiful girls in the world," was a success, and elevated the showgirl to a new kind of fame. At Carroll's

Theatre Restaurant, showgirls weren't pretty wallpaper for singers or jugglers; they didn't compete with fortune-tellers or comedians for attention. They were the heart of the show, the sexual engine that drew the crowds, and Carroll was as fiercely proud and protective of them as Hugh Hefner would one day be of his Playboy Bunnies. Carroll devised elaborate lists of do's and don'ts for his showgirls. He even made gentle fun of his obsession by featuring, in souvenir booklets, a beauty chart that called for no less than two dozen measurements and allowed patrons to see how they measured up to the club owner's exacting standards.

Carroll's approach triggered something of a range war, and clubs vied with each other to present the best, the most beautiful, the most unique, or sometimes simply the *most* in the way of showgirl power. Billy Rose made tall, leggy chorines his trademark, assembling a line of six-foot-and-over

In addition to the girls on stage, nightclubs hired pretty young women to fill other slots. There was the hatcheck girl, almost inevitably a Broadway or Hollywood hopeful who dreamed of one day telling her fans how she had started in this club or that and had been "discovered" by a producer or talent agent. There was also the pretty cigarette girl who roved the club in a short skirt, selling cigarettes from a tray slung around her neck like a feedsack. The hatcheck girl was protected within her cubicle, but the cigarette girl dealt with customers tableside and must have had to ward off many a pinch and pat in the course of an evening.

beauties who drew crowds to his Casa Mañana and Diamond Horseshoe clubs. To make his female customers feel tall and thin themselves, he featured a line of pretty and surprisingly agile hoofers, none of whom weighed less than three hundred pounds.

In New York, the epitome of showgirl glamour was reached in the forties and fifties, when the Latin Quarter and the Copacabana vied with each other to present the most dazzling and bespangled kicklines west of Paris.

For a few women, life in the chorus led to stardom. Peggy Hopkins Joyce, who married five times and wore on her arm a column of diamond and ruby bracelets she referred to as her "battle stripes," thought the chorus a fine alternative to marriage. "I have seen Earl Carroll and really his offer is quite flattering," she confided to her diary. "I shall make about five thousand dollars per week which is more than

Most memorable was the roving girl photographer. Like the cigarette girl, the girl photographer's outfit was usually short skirted, but her enormous, chunky camera lent her a modicum of protection—it reminded customers not only that its bearer was a professional but that, in a pinch, it could be used as a blocking

device or even, if things got rough, as a hurled missile. Before and during the show, the girl photographer went from table to table snapping pictures that were later developed and framed in a cardboard photo folder and sold, for a modest fee, as a souvenir memory of the night. Each club had its own stylish folder, and couples must have had fun collecting them.

Henri would give me, so why should I marry when I can make more myself than any man can give me?"

Peggy Hopkins Joyce was the exception, however. Most showgirls were simply hardworking entertainers who existed on the lower rungs of nightclub life. In late 1947, when a standing-room-only crowd at the Copa could bring the headwaiter one thousand dollars a week in tips, *Life* magazine noted that the average chorus girl earned fifty-five to seventy-five dollars for performing two shows a day in a six-day week. There were no job benefits to speak of and little in the way of job security. Many club owners considered "fresh faces" a must and maintained a revolving door policy when it came to hiring and firing dancers. Attention from stage-door Johnnies was ever present and could be a welcome perk or an annoying encumbrance, as the showgirls of Boston's Cocoanut Grove discovered on the night of November 28, 1942, when a fire, which erupted between shows, raced through the club in a matter of minutes. Several showgirls escaped wearing nothing but their flimsy costumes. Shivering from the cold and shock, the women huddled in the street—and still had to fend off advances from would-be admirers.

Of the thousands of women who danced across hundreds of nightclub floors, very few made it up and out of the ranks of the chorus. Some met tragic ends, such as Beryl Wallace, Earl Carroll's star and longtime love, who died alongside him in a 1948 plane crash; and Jean Spangler, whose murder more than fifty years ago is still listed as unsolved. Some transferred their talents to the new sensation, television, where the demand for variety dancers was constant; most drifted out of show business and into marriage, motherhood, and other pursuits, taking their memories and their glamour with them.

If they give me goose bumps, then I hire 'em.

—BILLY ROSE, ON HOW TO PICK A SHOWGIRL

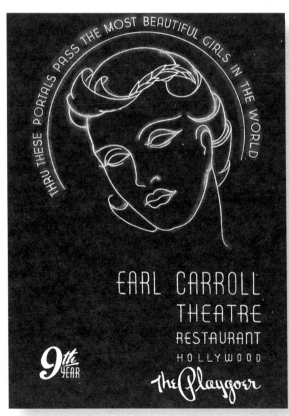

THRU THESE PORTALS PASS THE MOST BEAUTIFUL GIRLS IN THE WORLD

EARL CARROLL THEATRE RESTAURANT HOLLYWOOD

9th YEAR

The Playgoer

HARLEM NIGHTS

Without a doubt, one of the most dynamic nightclub entertainers to come out of America was Josephine Baker. Of course, to become Josephine Baker, the famously naked star had to leave America for the more libertine climes of Paris. In America, Baker had

no trouble getting work in various all-black revues and stage shows. But the idea of an African American becoming a solo act in mainstream clubs was unheard of. Even after her stardom was well established in Europe, the performer of such numbers as "The Banana Dance" found America unable to accept her on equal footing.

Baker's history with her country of origin is a small-scale version of America's larger ambivalence about black talent in general. While nightclubs evolved along one path in white America, they evolved along a different path in African American neighborhoods. White America enjoyed seeing troops of black singers and dancers perform in a prescribed way in white-owned clubs that catered to all-white audiences. There was an especial fascination with the exotic—and still "forbidden"—beauty of the African American woman. While places like the Ubangi Club and the Club Savannah unself-consciously advertised their "Negro revues," "Sepia Stage Shows," and chorus lines of "Beautiful Savannah Peaches," there was no hesitation in barring black patrons from clubs whose personnel and talent were all black.

In African American communities, and in Harlem in particular, a different type of nightclub evolved. Although there were plenty of showgirls and dancers in these clubs, there was a stronger emphasis on music—a music the likes of which had never been heard in the French Casino or

the Rainbow Room. Word soon crept out that hot jazz was being played north of 110th Street, and whites discovered the clubs along 133rd Street, the heart of Harlem.

How much conflict the white influx caused is open to debate. A Harlem community newspaper found the white interest in black nightlife

JOE HOWARD *presents* The New Spring Edition of
"ZANZABARABIAN NIGHTS"

Program

(IN ORDER OF APPEARANCE)

Introduction: CLAUDE HOPKINS
and His Orchestra

Your Host: PEE WEE MARQUETTE

BUNNY BRIGGS
in "CALIFORNIA SUNBEAM"
With the Zanziballadeers and the Zanzibeauts
WORDS AND MUSIC BY SAM H. STEPT

MARIE ELLINGTON
"Sophisticated Lady of Song"

HOWELL AND BOWSER
"America's Number Fun Comedy Team"

MAURICE ROCCO
in
"BOOGIE SAMBA"
With Nicky O'Daniels,
The Samba Boys and the Zanzibeauts

THE KING COLE TRIO
"The Top Singing and Musical Trio
of the Nation"

"UH HUH," HERE COMES
ROCHESTER
Jack Benny's "Shadow"

FINALE
"OCEANIC HOP"
"TILL WE MEET AGAIN
AT THE ZANZIBAR"
with the Entire Company

DANCING WITH
CLAUDE HOPKINS
AND HIS ORCHESTRA
AND
TED McRAE
AND HIS ORCHESTRA

THE STAFF
Conceived and Directed by Joe Howard
Dances and Staging by Clarence Robinson
Shoes: La Ray   Costumes: Madame Berthe
Musical Arrangements by Ted Murry
Orchestrations — Chappie Willit
Musical Director — Claude Hopkins
Talent Supervisor — Bill Kent
IF YOU WOULD LIKE TO HAVE THIS PROGRAM
MAILED TO A FRIEND, ADDRESS AND GIVE TO
YOUR WAITER... WE WILL PAY THE POSTAGE

"morbid," and there are anecdotes of white men being asked to leave clubs after asking black women to dance. But many club owners enjoyed the flow of white cash into their establishments, and, more often than not, clubs were open to whoever could pay to enter. At Dickie Wells's, in Harlem, mixed couples could even dance together without raising the eyebrows of fellow patrons.

Whatever integration existed in Harlem was rarely repeated in the white sections of town. There were, however, a few places that actively sought to end the status quo. Josephine Baker's manager, Ned Schuyler, went out of his way to book both black and white acts at his Copa City club in Miami. Baker herself played there in early 1951, yet was snubbed by Sherman Billingsley at the Stork Club only a few months later. Allegedly, Baker and her group were

seated but not served, and Billingsley, who prided himself on upscale elitism, was heard muttering, "Who the f- - - let her in?"

The most inventive blow against prejudice may have been struck by a club called Café Society in New York City. The name, like the place itself, was a riff on clubs like the Stork that took their vaunted elitism far too seriously. Operating out of a basement in Greenwich Village, the place became so popular it soon opened a branch on the swank—and largely white—East Fifty-eighth Street near Park Avenue. The addition, which became known as Café Society Uptown, must have been deeply satisfying to those who had long been looking for a way to challenge the city's complex and invisible color lines.

With its clever slogan, "The Wrong Place for the Right People," Café Society became a favorite with progressive artists and writers, not to mention lovers of hot jazz. It also became the place where, in 1939, Billie Holiday regularly sang the haunting "Strange Fruit." The song was always her closing number, and the moment before she began to sing it, all activity in the club would cease. Waiters and busboys would return to their stations and the room would go dark. A pinpoint of light would shine on Holiday as she sang, and the club would be dark again on her finishing note. No matter how great the applause, she never came back for a bow or encore following the song, preferring to let the song's painful images and haunting notes linger with the audience.

The Cotton Club

Of all the bright and dazzling black clubs, none sparkled as brightly or cut such a wide path through the American psyche as the Cotton Club. As with many such clubs of the era, the term "black" is only partially accurate. The waiters and talent were black. The audience, like the owners, was white.

The club opened in the fall of 1923 in the old Douglas Theater building on 142nd Street and Lenox Avenue in Harlem. The chief owner was Owen Madden, a professional racketeer

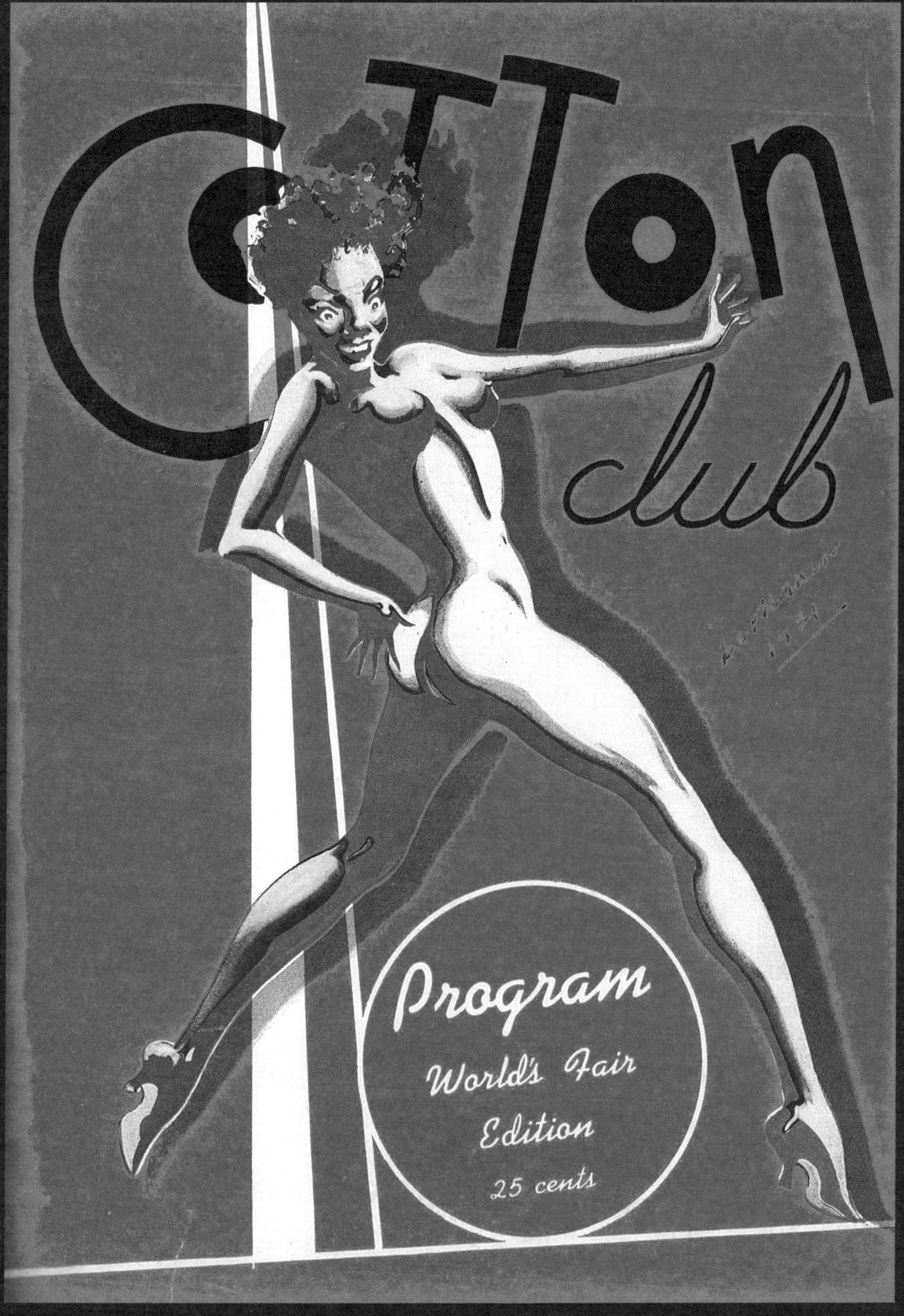
Cotton club
Program
World's Fair Edition
25 cents

from Chicago. He planned the club from prison and was in jail throughout much of his tenure as owner. Madden's sole interest in the club was to cash in on the white interest in all things African. To make the white crowd feel at home, he expanded the floor space to seat seven hundred and erected artificial palms. The menu was a multicultural meltdown featuring steak, lobster, and Chinese and Mexican cuisine alongside neighborhood favorites like barbecued ribs and fried chicken. The inclusion of Harlem fare wasn't to make locals feel at home but to give the Park Avenue crowd a chance to sample authentic African American cooking. Blacks were explicitly barred as patrons; there were no exceptions.

In the Cotton Club, Madden conceived of a venue that was run like a downtown club but with the exotic talent found uptown. The stage show might be wild, but the audience could never be. Good behavior was

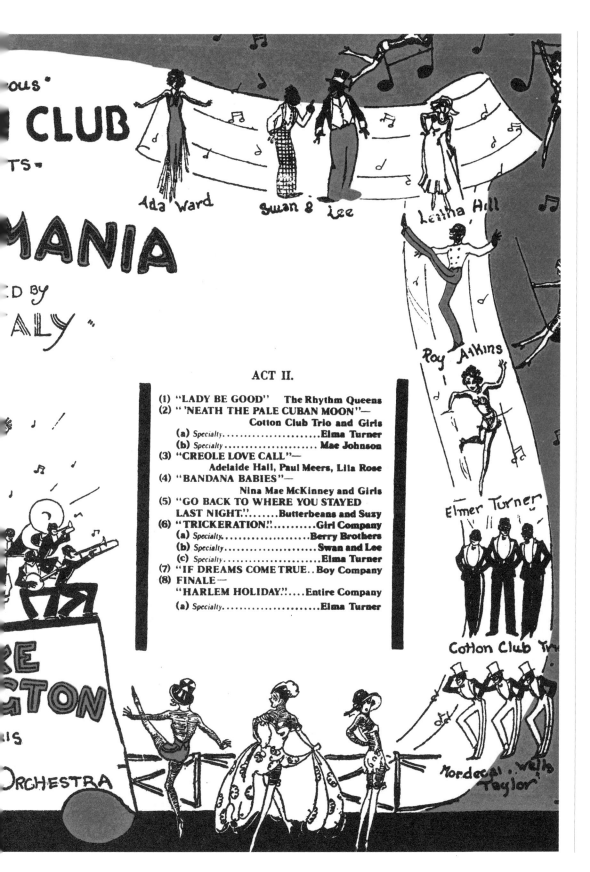

Ada Ward

Swan & Lee

Leitha Hill

Roy Atkins

Elmer Turner

Cotton Club Tr...

Mordecai..Wells Taylor

ACT II.

(1) "LADY BE GOOD"   The Rhythm Queens
(2) " 'NEATH THE PALE CUBAN MOON"—
  Cotton Club Trio and Girls
  (a) Specialty..................Elma Turner
  (b) Specialty.................. Mae Johnson
(3) "CREOLE LOVE CALL"—
  Adelaide Hall, Paul Meers, Lila Rose
(4) "BANDANA BABIES"—
  Nina Mae McKinney and Girls
(5) "GO BACK TO WHERE YOU STAYED
  LAST NIGHT.".......Butterbeans and Suzy
(6) "TRICKERATION."..........Girl Company
  (a) Specialty....................Berry Brothers
  (b) Specialty....................Swan and Lee
  (c) Specialty....................Elma Turner
(7) "IF DREAMS COME TRUE..Boy Company
(8) FINALE—
  "HARLEM HOLIDAY."....Entire Company
  (a) Specialty....................Elma Turner

expected, especially when performers were on stage. Customers who made too much noise during the shows were warned once and then asked to leave. The club also kept its prices as high, and perhaps a bit higher, than those of the downtown clubs. There was a three-dollar cover charge, bootleg beer was a dollar a bottle, and orange juice a dollar and a quarter per glass. The customers didn't seem to mind; in fact, they seemed to enjoy paying for the privilege of being in a "real" black club. Waiters and musicians found they could make a good living convincing white patrons that it was customary to tip more in Harlem than downtown.

Another factor in the club's success was its schedule. The late show at the Cotton Club began after the late shows at the other clubs were over, allowing performers from other clubs to see the show. The Cotton Club soon became the "in" spot for people like Jimmy Durante,

Milton Berle, Eleanor Holm, Billy Rose, Eddie Cantor, and Paul Whiteman. Once this became known, the usual crowd of celebrity seekers streamed north as well.

Yet what made the crowds come at all, and kept them coming back, was the talent. From the start, the Cotton Club offered a superior show. Madden and his syndicate wanted performers who could deliver the kind of "primitive" and "exotic" revue white patrons expected, and within these narrow parameters black performers hammered more talent and originality into a floor show than had ever been seen on a nightclub stage.

Like the splashy downtown clubs, the Cotton Club had its own chorus line. To audition, girls had to stand over five-foot-six and be under twenty-one years old. They also had to be light skinned, a requirement that didn't apply to the club's male performers. To pass the audition, young women had to be able to sing as well as dance. The Cotton Club placed more emphasis on these skills than other clubs did, and, as a result, the club's chorus line was one of the most talented in the city.

In addition to its chorus, the Cotton Club, like its rivals downtown, featured male and female vocalists and dance teams who could rumba, mambo, and tango. Then there were the bands. The club's original ensemble, Andy Preer's Missourians (also known as the Cotton Club Syncopators), was competent but not outstanding. When Preer died in 1927, club owners began searching for a replacement band. They settled on a group called the Washingtonians, which had just finished a yearlong stint at the Kentucky Club in Times Square and was then on the road in Philadelphia. The switch was an instant success, and the group, which soon took the name of its leader and became known as the Duke Ellington Band, made the Cotton Club *the* hot spot in Harlem.

While the Cotton Club previously had been doing well with the white patrons it courted, the new band sent its popularity over the top. Ellington and his music thrilled the audience as his predecessor had not. A local radio station even began broadcasting from the club. When the broadcast was picked up by the CBS network, the Cotton Club became a national mecca. People came to see it from all over the country and all over the world. Within a year, Ellington had become the club's chief drawing card, wielding enough clout to get the club's manager to admit friends and relatives of performers as well as prominent African Americans. The all-important color line was finally breached. White patrons didn't seem to notice, or if they did notice they didn't care. The club remained as popular as ever, though "ordinary" black people were still denied admittance.

Duke Ellington made the Cotton Club world famous, and the Cotton Club did the same for Ellington. In addition to recording contracts, he and his band soon were booked for Broadway musicals and movies. While they were in Hollywood in 1930 making *Check and Double Check,* another band had to be found to fill their spot. Their replacement was playing at another Harlem spot called the Crazy Cat Club, and the leader of the new band was named Cab Calloway.

To bill Cab Calloway merely as a bandleader would be to miss the

mark by a mile. Calloway was a phenomenon in his own right, a whirling dervish who spun from the orchestra to the microphone and back again and always seemed on the brink of completely losing control. Spoofing the dress styles of the day, Calloway moved from tailored tails to an elegantly exaggerated zoot suit, complete with broad-brimmed hat and a swinging watch chain that reached almost to his ankles. How he performed without tripping remains one of the mysteries of the era.

Audiences loved to watch Calloway and enjoyed the rich, low-down blues music that was his band's specialty. It was at the Cotton Club one night that Calloway acquired his famous nickname. In the midst of his well-known rendition of "Minnie the Moocher," he forgot the words. When it was time for him to join in, he simply shouted "hi-de-ho" into the microphone. The crowd loved it and shouted "hi-de-ho" right back at him. Calloway soon became known as the Hi-De-Ho Man, and those three simple syllables summed up the whole what-the-hell, isn't-this-a-hoot atmosphere of the Harlem glory days.

When Ellington and his band returned to the Cotton Club, Calloway was hired by a rival nightclub, the Club Plantation. It wasn't long until the Plantation burned down under

mysterious circumstances that had Owen Madden's fingerprints all over them. In late 1930, when Ellington wanted more creative freedom and again left the Cotton Club, Calloway was brought back. The two bands began alternating on a regular basis, and standing-room-only audiences could be counted on for either one.

By the thirties, the Cotton Club had established itself as the leading nightclub for musical entertainment. Harold Arlen and Ted Koehler were hired to write music for the revues, and the lavish floor shows were costing some four thousand dollars a week to stage. In 1932 a singer named Lucille Wilson auditioned at the club. Arlen and Koehler were so impressed with her that they persuaded management to drop its policy of employing only light-skinned women. Wilson, who later married Louis Armstrong, was hired on the proviso that she would be let go if the audience complained. No one did; they loved Wilson, and she sang at the club for the next eight years.

In 1933, the singer Ethel Waters returned to New York after a long period on the road. Arlen and Koehler were eager to get her to sing one of their new songs. Waters listened to the number and agreed, provided she could sing it her way—in a simplified stage setting with minimal orchestration, relying on her voice and emotion to carry the song. The number, "Stormy Weather," became an instant sensation, and even people who weren't club-goers beat a path to Harlem.

For the next several years, Waters periodically returned to the club to sing her showstopper. One night, Waters overheard one of the showgirls imitating her doing the song. Waters made her presence known and the embarrassed showgirl began apologizing. Waters swept the apology aside and told the girl she should forget about dancing and develop her terrific singing voice. That showgirl was Lena Horne.

Waters, Horne, and others made the Cotton Club world famous. Nevertheless, the Depression eventually took its toll on the club. Unemployment rates reached 80 percent in Harlem, and white people no longer found it such a gay place to visit. (One can only imagine how local residents felt toward people who continued to come to their neighborhood to dine and dance when they themselves could scarcely afford to eat.) The Cotton Club closed on February 16, 1936, and began looking to relocate farther south. The club found new quarters on the top floor of a building at Broadway and Forty-eighth Street, former home of the Palais Royal, the Harlem Club, and the Ubangi Club.

The downtown Cotton Club opened its doors in the fall of 1936. Though the club lasted only four years, its shows were more lavish and boasted more famous names than ever. Ellington and Calloway continued to rotate bookings, and Louis Armstrong came to play. Bill (Bojangles) Robinson performed his famous stair dance, floating so lightly up the stairs that viewers often claimed he possessed the ability to levitate. Steppin' Fetchit, a canny genius who made a fortune fulfilling white folks' naive stereotypes, agreed to perform—at a price that nearly bankrupted the place. Sister Rosetta Tharpe and Dorothy Dandridge and her sisters made their debuts, too. The club, which earlier had introduced a dance called the Suzy-Q, started a new sensation with a dance called the Boogie Woogie. For the inauguration of the club's second downtown season, Ellington came back, and for the first time in nightclub history all the show's major numbers were written by African Americans.

Initially, the downtown club was a smash, bringing in an average of thirty thousand dollars a week. But the bite of the Depression was deep and long-lasting. Even people who once had thousands in the bank were finally broke. An ennui settled over the country, and after a few years the club's revues lost the fast-paced sparkle for which they were famous. And in a way, the Cotton Club suffered from its own success. It had blurred color lines by showcasing talent too good to be ignored. As a result, black performers found it easier to get jobs on the stage and in movies. The Cotton Club was no longer the only place people could go to see black talent, and the club lost its franchise. Like many nightclubs that couldn't quite make it through the Depression, the Cotton Club closed for good in June of 1940. One measure of its fame can be found in the fact that today, more than sixty years after its passing, almost everyone still knows of the Cotton Club.

THE ELEGANT ROOMS

Not all nightclubs aimed to be the largest and loudest. Some merchandised a far more restrained version of the Big Night Out. These clubs were most often tucked into the city's most elegant hotels or lofted atop downtown office buildings. Instead of carnival-like names, their titles suggested safe and stately enclaves of Victorian sensibility, usually with the word "Room" or "Roof" worked in at the end. In New York, there were the Wedgewood and Empire Rooms at the Waldorf Astoria, as well as its elegant Starlight Roof, where Xavier Cugat, Tony Bennett, and Victor Borge entertained. There was the Commodore's Century Room, and the Cotillion Room at the Hotel Pierre, as well as the Astor Roof, where Harry James and his orchestra sprayed notes into the air like a shower of stars. Boston's elegant spot was the Oval Room at the Copley Plaza, where Morton Downey was a regular head-

BLUE ROOM, THE ROOSEVE

NEW ORLEANS, LOUISIANA

liner. In New Orleans, the Roosevelt Hotel's Blue Room had chandeliers the size of grand pianos and marble columns supporting the indigo-and-white ceiling.

Rooms like these didn't have showgirls, they had female vocalists. They didn't have bands, they had orchestras. Instead of kinetic vaudevillians there were ballroom dancers and singing quartets. For frivolity, the occasional magician might be thrown into the mix. Even when an edge of ethnic-themed exotica threatened, these clubs kept it well in check. New York's Blackstone did have a Balinese Room, but, lest there be any doubt, the club's table card assured customers they were in for a night of "sophisticated entertainment." As further proof of its bona fides, the club also reminded patrons they were in the presence of "America's only copper dance floor." The beauty of this type of nightclub was that almost any city could have one.

Balinese ROOM

FEATURING...

JOHNNY DUFFY

and HIS ORCHESTRA

SONGS BY...

PATTI CLAYTON

•

Sophisticated Entertainment

•

America's Only Copper Dance Floor

•

Luncheon • Dinner • Supper
Served Daily

No Minimum or Cover Charge

The Blackstone

While extravaganzas like the Copacabana, the French Casino, and the Tropicana required a large and constant customer volume to stay in business, the elegant rooms operated on a more modest scale. A city too small to support a Latin Quarter or a Cocoanut Grove could still have, as Cleveland did, a Vogue Room tucked into the Hollenden Hotel. Here Cleveland got its first glimpse of the local boy from nearby Steubenville, Dean Martin.

The idea of the elegant room was transported and translated across America. Eventually it became the ubiquitous local ballroom, the place where proms and cotillions were held, where the children of Storm Lake, Iowa, could go to the Cobblestone to hear Glenn Miller and the Dorsey brothers as they swooped through corn country on a coast-to-coast caravan.

The Rainbow Room

Elegant even by the elegant-room standard, no club became as famous—or lasted as long—as New York's Rainbow Room. From its opening night in 1934 to its final closing some sixty years later, the club symbolized the epitome of champagne living. Located on the sixty-fifth floor of the then-new Radio City, the room was a sleek study in understated grace; there were no gilded moldings or showy fake palms. The large, high-ceilinged room was walled with mirrors and polished metal fretwork. Tables, lifted on grass-green terraces, ringed a dance floor that revolved like a slow, lazy lagoon. Even the most urbane of urban sophisticates was dazzled by the white-glove demeanor of the place.

Another Headline Attraction On Our "Parade of Stars", in a Brilliant, Variety Stage Show.

★ OPENING TUESDAY, JULY 20th ★

None Other Than The Celebrated & Talented Vocal Sensation

DOLLY DAWN FAMED "NBC" SINGING STAR of STAGE, SCREEN, RECORDS, RADIO & TELEVISION

• IN PERSON • DIRECT FROM THE "COPACABANA"

"Orchids" - from Walter Winchell ! ! !

CLUB RHAPSODY

❖ FACING THE CATARACTS ❖

NIAGARA FALLS, N.Y.

FOR RESERVATIONS: PHONE 2-7581 & 2-9513

The Rainbow Room opened in the midst of the Depression and succeeded by appealing to the select few with money to spend. Unlike many other clubs, which lowered their prices and still went under, the Rainbow Room charged more than other clubs and was full every night. Inside its glossy walls, one would never guess unemployment was running at a rate of 21.7 percent. Evening gowns were de rigueur for the ladies, as was black tie for the men. Orchestras, drawn from the more refined ranks of swing, included Ray Noble and his orchestra, imported from London, and Glenn Gray's Casa Loma. The gypsy fortune-teller, a nightclub standard everywhere, was billed as an "Egyptian Mystic" at the Rainbow Room.

The Rainbow Room is one of the few night resorts in the world that really looks like a tank-town movie fan's idea of the elegant life.

—FORTUNE, 1936

With all this glass, steel, silk, and satin, the rude fads of the hoi polloi seemed jarringly out of place. So it was that, in 1937, the Rainbow Room banned the dance craze sweeping the nation, the Big Apple. The dance, a group gyration born at the Big Apple Night Club in Columbia, South Carolina, wasn't without its hazards; there were reports of balconies and dance floors that had collapsed under the weight of people doing the dance. The Rainbow Room claimed it banished the Big Apple out of concern for its patrons' health and safety, but chances are they also agreed with the college professor, quoted in *Life* magazine, who found the dance "fun but crude."

Despite the high prices and steady stream of well-heeled patrons, the Rainbow Room was not a moneymaker. From its earliest days, rumors of large-scale losses circulated almost continuously, although these didn't seem to bother anyone. In chronicling the early years of the nightclub era, Stanley Walker wrote in 1933 that the whole fantastic business prospered because, "wealthy men from out of town visited the clubs for appalling orgies of spending and drinking, and most of them seemed to think it was worth the cost." The same might be said of the Rockefellers, part-owners of the Rainbow Room. For years they poured money into the place like champagne and seemed, like everyone else, more than happy with the result.

The Rainbow Room

P R O G R A M

Dinner Show 8:30 p. m. Supper Show 12:15 a. m.

PRESENTS

GLENN GRAY and his CASA LOMA ORCHESTRA
featuring PEE WEE HUNT and KENNY SARGENT

SHEILA BARRETT MILDRED MONSON
Satirical Mimic Song Stylist

JACK HOLLAND and JUNE HART
Dancers

NANCY NOLAND GALI-GALI
Pianist and Organist Egyptian Mystifier

NANO RODRIGO
and his Tango and Rhumba Orchestra

No Couvert Charge for Dinner Guests remaining after 10 p. m.
Except Saturdays and Holiday Eves $1.50
A Couvert of $1.50 is charged after 10:30 p. m.; Saturdays and Holiday Eves $2.50

ROCKEFELLER CENTER ROOF ★

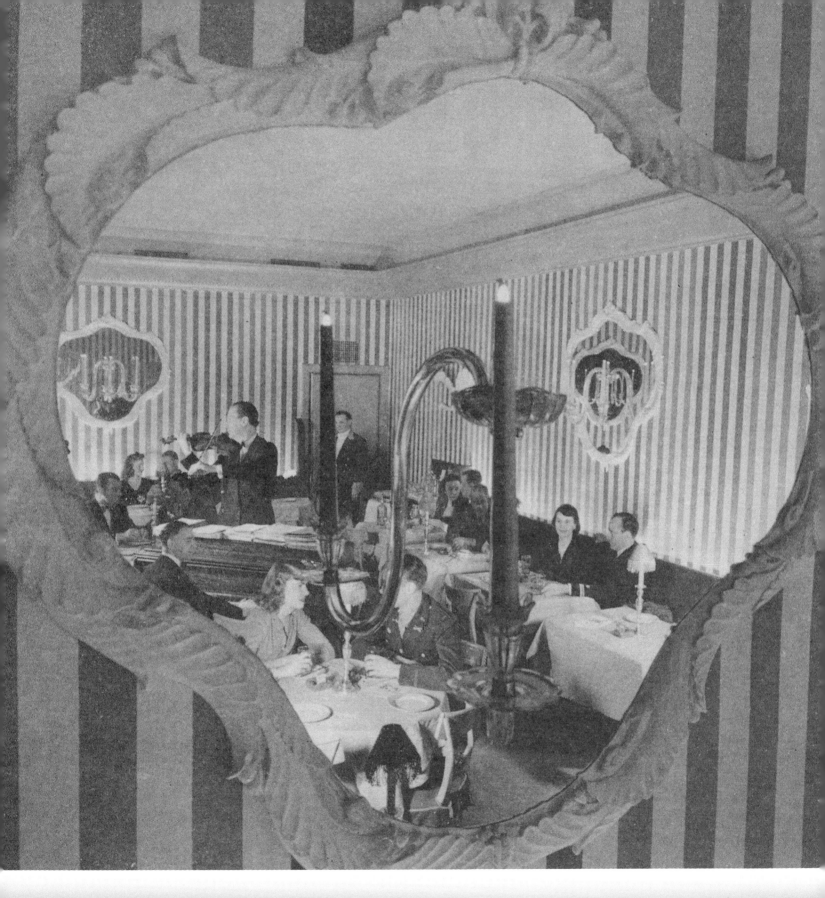

NON-NIGHTCLUB NIGHTCLUBS

The Stork Club
and
El Morocco

There were no revues, no showgirls, no jugglers, no comedians, and no professional rumba teams. There were bands and dancing, but the real action took place at the crowded tables and banquettes and along the polished bars. Technically speaking, New York's Stork Club and El Morocco might not even have been nightclubs. But no one was speaking technically. For thousands of people in thousands of places, no two names conjured more vividly the bright, floating bubble of nightclub life than these two clubs.

The Stork Club and El Morocco were each other's chief competition. They also resembled each other in many ways. Both owed a good share of their success to the personalities of their hosts. Both distinguished themselves from dozens of other dine-and-dance clubs by creating an aura of exclusivity. Both were among the most expensive watering holes in New York, whose high prices and velvet-rope lines were calculated to inspire longing in the very throngs they kept at bay. Both clubs thrived on publicity and both published their own newsletters—*Stork Club Talk* and El Morocco's *No News*.

Once inside, patrons of both clubs found themselves in a protected haven, a sophisticated game preserve where the celebrated classes could mingle with each other—safe from the hurly-burly of the streets—and be catered to by a flying phalanx of waiters, busboys, and barmen. Both clubs boasted plenty of well-known faces and newsworthy names, but at the Stork and El Morocco, the names and faces belonged to the customers, not the entertainment.

The Stork was the older of the two clubs, but its first incarnation, on New York's speakeasy-clogged West Fifty-eighth Street, was hardly promising. Soon after the club opened, the

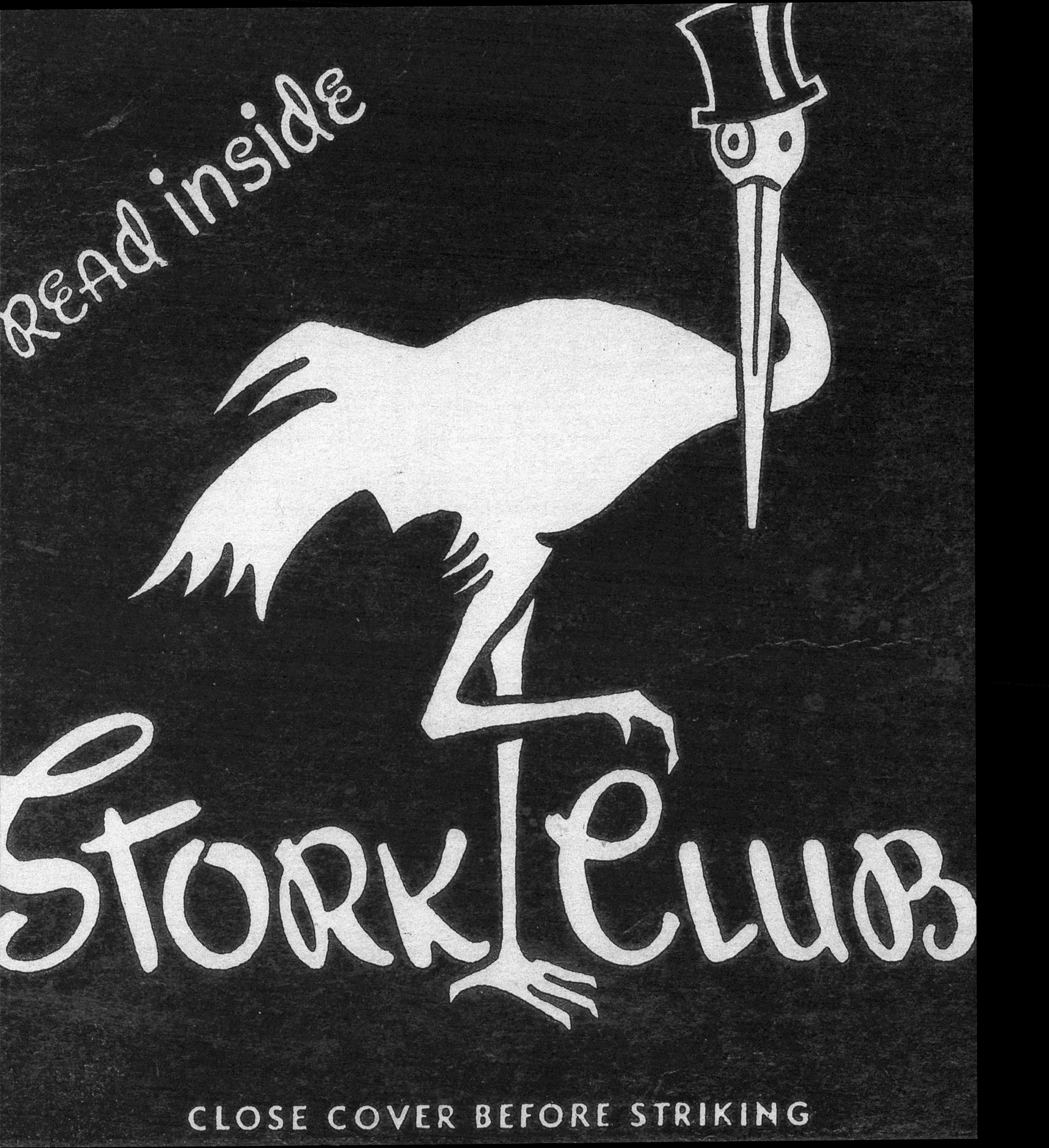
READ inside
STORK CLUB
CLOSE COVER BEFORE STRIKING

We agreed
El Morocco
was the base of
the idle, untal-
ented rich.
The Stork
was the race-
track and show-
place of the
Meritocracy,
the winners, the
career people of
both sexes.

—ERNEST CUNEO,
WALTER WINCHELL'S LAWYER

Beautiful women are the only decoration worth a damn in a nightclub.

—SHERMAN BILLINGSLEY

crash of '29 reduced the flood of paying customers to a trickle. Host Sherman Billingsley, a fresh-faced bootlegger from Oklahoma, tried to keep the place afloat by appealing to a higher-grade clientele. He removed prostitutes, gamblers, and spittoons from the premises. He erected an awning, gentrified the decor, and displayed his illegal liquor in bottles instead of pouring bathtub gin from pitchers hidden beneath the counter.

But his efforts weren't enough. The club was on the verge of closing when fellow club owner Tex Guinan performed a near miracle. Famous for her "Hello, suckers" greeting and her necklace made of padlocks (in tribute to the number of times her clubs had been raided), Tex was one of the more colorful characters of the day. She was also a friend of Walter Winchell's, and to help Billingsley she suggested to the newsman that he give the Stork some play in his column. When Winchell, America's most influential gossip columnist,

C R I M E   B E A T

From the beginning, it was supposed that nightclubs had their shady and nefarious side. For the most part, this supposition was correct. Born of the rough-and-tumble years of Prohibition, established to circumvent the rigors of the Volstead Act, the nightclub had a natural appeal to criminals looking for business. Many club owners, including the Stork Club's Sherman Billingsley, were former bootleggers. Others embraced an even broader spectrum of crime. Racketeer Larry Fay, a partner in many New York clubs including El Fay, Fay's Follies, and Les Ambassadeurs, had been arrested more than four dozen times. At the bottom of the heap was Club Chantee in New York, where the staff included "Shuffles" Goldberg and Jake and Leon Kramer, known throughout the underworld as the greatest safecrackers in history. Their employer and the club manager, Richard Reese Whitmore, was eventually hanged for murder. Fortunately, the place burned to the ground in 1926.

A more discreet and more common practice was for a club to have a "clean" manager, someone with no criminal record, who fronted the business. Behind this legitimate facade, the club might have a matrix of partners and investors whose records were less than pristine. So complex and confusing were these arrangements, with front men for front men and holding companies within holding companies, that it was often impossible to determine exactly who owned the clubs—which was, of course, extremely convenient when things ran afoul of the law.

Especially in the early days, nightclub operators found it nearly impossible to run a completely legal establishment. When Billy Rose's first endeavor, the Backstage Club, proved successful, a bunch of wise guys waltzed in and announced themselves as his new partners. Rose decided to avoid the problem by serving no booze at his next establishment, the Fifth Avenue Club; but without the allure of bathtub gin, the club was a failure. By the time he opened the Casino de Paris, Rose had come up with a plan: This time, when the mob approached him, Rose complained to his good friend Bernard Barruch, who put in a call to his good friend J. Edgar Hoover. Whom Hoover called is unknown, but Rose was never bothered again.

Like everyone else, professional criminals also enjoyed being part of the audience. According to Jerry Lewis, it was common for the heads of New York's leading crime families to bring their wives and children to the Copacabana on Sunday evenings to see the show. Their conduct was perfectly polite and aboveboard, making the next day's headlines implicating these same men in all manner of mayhem seem all the more jarring.

Of course, not all crime occurred outside the clubs; some was created by the clubs themselves. In 1944, New York mayor Fiorello La Guardia accused several of the city's most famous clubs of tax evasion. The Copacabana and La Vie Parisienne were both on the list, but the biggest offender by far was the Stork Club. The Stork's alleged tab for owed taxes totaled over one hundred and eighty thousand dollars. According to the city, the Stork had developed a neat system for skimming: Waiters laid the bill on the table face down, presenting the customer with the back of the bill and a falsely inflated total. The Stork banked on the fact that no one stylish enough to patronize the Stork would stoop so low as to look at the front of the check. Hence the club paid taxes on the lesser, correct amount shown on the front and pocketed—tax-free—the overage provided by customers who paid the inflated amount on the back. The suit outlasted La Guardia's term as mayor, dragged through the courts for half a decade, and cost the Stork over one hundred thousand dollars. Billingsley simply didn't care: from a publicity standpoint, the ongoing brouhaha was worth its weight in gold.

proclaimed the Stork "New York's New Yorkiest" club, people turned up to see what all the fuss was about. Before Winchell's help, Billingsley had been spending ten thousand dollars a month to keep the doors open. Afterward, the club cleared ten thousand dollars a week.

In 1931, the newly profitable Stork left the West Side for a ritzier location, eventually establishing itself at 3 East Fifty-third Street. Winchell made the club his headquarters and established himself as columnist-in-residence at table fifty. One night at the club, Lana Turner and Artie Shaw told him they were getting a divorce. Another night, Grace Kelly stopped by to announce her engagement to Prince Rainier of Monaco. Winchell spent so much time at the Stork he even had his favorite sandwich added to the menu, the "Chicken Hamburger à la Winchell."

The same year the Stork came to the East Side, El Morocco (known to insiders as Elmo's) opened on East Fiftieth Street. Like the Stork Club, El Morocco was very much the creation of its host, John Perona. Older than Billingsley, the dark, dapper, Italian-born Perona brought an old-world ethos to his club. While Billingsley cultivated a new aristocracy of entertainers, athletes, writers, and politicians, Perona courted an older, monied crowd, heirs of fortunes made in the early days of the century. Before El Morocco, Perona had run the Bath Club, transforming it into the seemingly impossible—an elegant New York speakeasy. With El Morocco, he hoped to create a club whose appeal would outlast Prohibition.

Not surprisingly, regulars of the two clubs fell into separate camps and squared off like Montagues and Capulets. El Morocco's supporters found the Stork's patrons showy and arriviste, while patrons of the Stork felt that they were part of an elect meritocracy.

Being a regular at either club was a good thing. Both Billingsley and Perona believed in the personal touch, greeting favored customers like old friends and dispensing many little perks and privileges along the way. For the "elect," cover charges were waived, as were dinner and bar bills. The "unelect" paid cover charges and full price for everything. Table hoppers sought to evade the cover fee by drifting from group to group. Who was "in" and who was "out" was entirely up to the host, and

Bartenders—Waiters—Captains

Watch me close, keep your eyes on me when I am at your service station. If I put my hand up to my ear that means that I want to get away from the party I am with, so you come over to me and say Mr. Billingsley there is a phone call for you in the office. I never like to stand at the bar so anytime you see me standing at the bar talking to any customer call me to the telephone.

If I am on a stool don't call me unless I put my hand on my ear.

—MEMO TO THE TROOPS FROM SHERMAN BILLINGSLEY

"EL MOROCCO" NO-NEWS

Fortune magazine noted that one of Perona's chief trade secrets was "an elastic cover charge, which he used to separate the chic from the goats." Both Billingsley and Perona gave gifts to favorite customers, sending ties to the men and compacts and perfume vials to the ladies; each item bore the logo of the respective club. Favored customers also were permitted use of the house telephones (usually rushed to the table by an accommodating waiter), and the best customers at the Stork could avail themselves of the club's all-night bank, barbershop, and gym.

The main room at El Morocco was meant to suggest an outing to Marrakech—a very clean, civilized, and climate-controlled Marrakech. The ceiling was an artificial sky of the deepest blue. Lantern-lit palm trees leaned from the sides of the room and arabesque grillwork decorated the walls. Booths and banquettes were upholstered with zebra-striped upholstery executed in smoky blue and white, a motif that quickly became famous. (To Billingsley's great annoyance, any publicity shot taken at El Morocco was sure to show the distinctive Rorschach zebra stripe, leaving no doubt in the public's mind as to where the photo was snapped. This ingenious stroke, whether planned or accidental, proved more valuable to the club than a hefty advertising budget ever would have been.) For patrons craving the traditional, El Morocco also had a candlelit Champagne Room, whose striped walls, strolling violinists, and mirrored wall sconces conjured up the good old days of the Austro-Hungarian empire.

The appointments at the Stork were sparer but no less elegant. The main room was a cozily padded cell, an L-shaped space that could seat one hundred and sixty patrons. The walls were paneled with mirrors and dark blue velvet, the ceiling covered with heavy yellow and gray satin. There were crystal chandeliers and a fifteen-by-twenty-foot oval dance floor. More spartan but far more coveted was the famous Cub Room, better known as the "snub room." No ordinary patron set foot within its walls. Here the big names of the day relaxed, drank, and played gin rummy. The Cub Room was where Marilyn Monroe and Joe DiMaggio went during the early days of their marriage, where one could see J. Edgar Hoover as well as the infamous Frank Costello, the duke and duchess of Windsor, and, years later, a bright young senator from New York named John F. Kennedy.

Whatever they lacked in floor shows and mambo teams, the Stork Club and El Morocco made up for by being indisputably "in." For years these reigned as the places to be, a fact affirmed by the crowds who hovered outside, waiting for a glimpse of those who came and went.

HAVANAMANIA!

ANA GLORIA
& ROLANDO
Queen and King
of Mambo

TROPICANA

HAVANA - CUBA

"A Paradise Under the Stars"

The advertisements promised "paradise under the stars," and they weren't far wrong. Once upon a time, Cuba's tropical climate, thrilling music, and excellent rum coalesced to create a glittering playground for grown-ups. After all, Cuba was the birthplace of the mambo, the rumba, and the cha-cha, and home to elegant hotels, wandering celebrities, and icy daiquiris. For tourists in those halcyon days, getting to Cuba was a form of entertainment itself. Cruise ships did a brisk business. Some lines offered to ferry people's cars as well as their luggage, and in the fifties a four-day–three-night outing aboard the SS *Florida* could be had for well under one hundred dollars. Those with less time or more distance to cover might fly Cubana airlines direct from New York, Madrid, and other major cities, or take one of the special "dinner flights" from Miami, leaving in the early evening and returning the next morning. On some routes, a tuxedo-clad pianist kept the first-class section entertained.

In Havana, the nightclubs and casinos were in full swing. Gambling was legal, and many establishments featured the alluring trifecta of excellent food, casino gaming, and floor shows. Some clubs, such as the Kursaal and the Zombie, emphasized their criollo spirit, while others, like the Sans Souci and the Tokio, suggested the international and the exotic. Even small clubs were sure to have a rumba team; the flashier places blended Cuban-born dancers and musicians with international headliners such as Dorothy Lamour, Lena Horne, and Maurice Chevalier, all of whom played Havana's Montmartre in the summer of 1956.

The Tropicana

In the lush atmosphere that was Havana, the lushest club of all was the Tropicana. Opened in 1939, it quickly became famous throughout the world. It was at the Tropicana that showgirls raised to a high art the skill of wearing towering headdresses and little else. And it was here, in 1943, that Perez Prado introduced a sensational, exuberantly acrobatic dance called the mambo. The mambo was eventually exported to America, but not before it was toned down—Yankees found the dance, with its voodoo origins, distressingly athletic and almost violent. Besides mambo dancers and a mambo orchestra, the Tropicana also had rumba dancers and a rumba orchestra. Over two hundred chorus girls, reputed to be the most beautiful women in Cuba, staged a lavish floor show twice a night.

To enter the Tropicana, one pulled into a curving driveway flanked by the club on one side and a large fountain on the other. At the center of the fountain was a sleek, modern statue of a dancer on point, her brief skirt rippling faintly in the tropical night. Inside the door, beyond the lobby, was the Gaming Room, where one could play chemin de fer or blackjack and where the spindle of the roulette wheel was a miniature replica of the ballerina in the outside fountain. The same ballerina icon was again repeated on the club's swizzle sticks, cocktail napkins, and matches.

After its first profitable decade, the Tropicana added the Crystal Arch Room, an enormous terrace covered by a roof of magnificent sweeping arches. Here diners could watch the stage show or, if that paled, gaze directly up at the stars. In the fifties, when nightclubs in America were beginning to look a bit dated and overblown, the Crystal Arch Room had the ambitious, modern feel of a flight-hangar-sized boomerang. People came from all over the world to see it, but most came from prosperous, postwar

Showtime at... TROPICANA

Every Night... 2

unforgetable! Two lavish revues each night with world-famous stars. Two wonderful orchestras have you swaying to rhumba rhythms or mambos at first beat of the bongo. And lovely Latin showgirls... ahhh! Don't miss it!

RESERVATIONS: PHONE B-4544

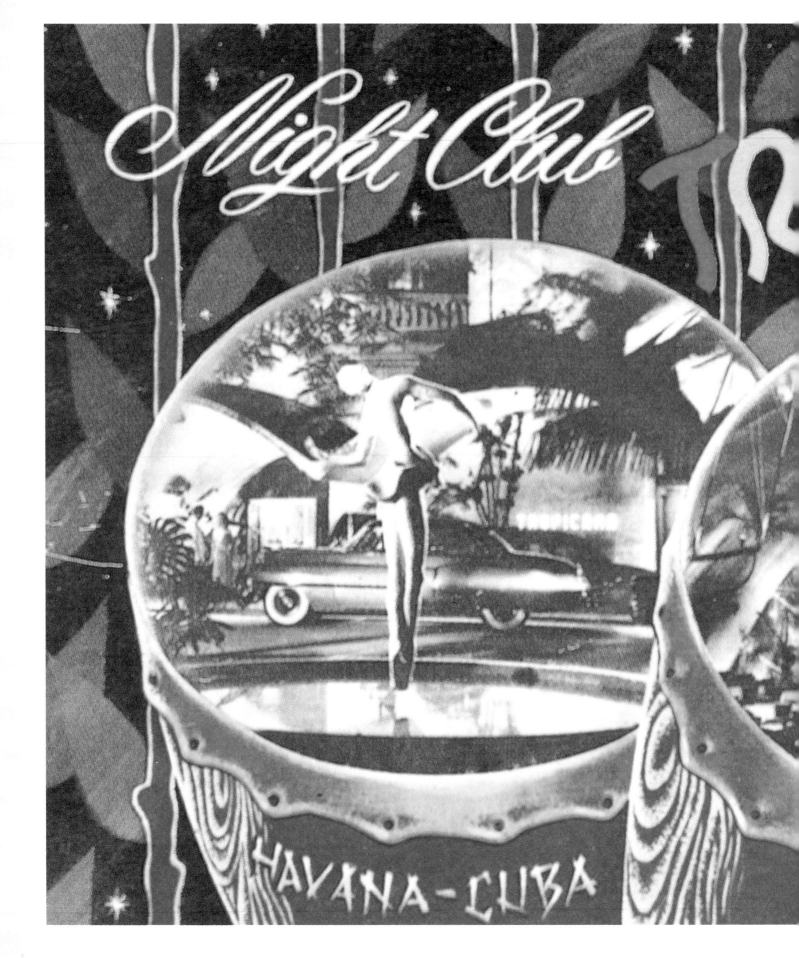

America. Though the Tropicana was frequented by Americans in general, it was so popular in Hollywood in particular that many celebrities had their own favorite tables at the club. Without the faintest trace of irony, the Tropicana of the fifties described itself in its advertising as "America's most beautiful nightclub."

The chill that descended on Cuban-American relations in the wake of Fidel Castro's rise to power in 1959 effectively pulled the plug on American junketing but not, ironically, on the Tropicana itself. Despite a revolution, economic upheaval, and nationalization, the club has lasted into the twenty-first century. The gambling, food, and magnificent location are gone, but the glitz has remained. If one is in Havana today, it's still possible to catch a floor show and watch as chorus girls in swaying, illuminated head-dresses take to the stage to perform the club's showstopping "Dance of the Chandeliers."

THE SOUTH HEADS NORTH

Long before the Revolution, Cuba's chief exports, dance and music, already were being freely exported. Attempts to introduce the rumba to the United States were made as early as 1913, but it didn't catch on until 1923, when Emil Coleman brought musicians and a rumba dance team to New York. Coleman, one of the most popular bandleaders of the era, did much to spread the rumba's fame. Two years later, the first full-fledged Latin-themed club, El Chico, opened in New York's Greenwich Village.

I would rather play "Chiquita Banana"

and have my swimming pool than play Bach and starve.

—XAVIER CUGAT

By far the most influential exporter of the Latin craze was bandleader Xavier Cugat. Born in Barcelona, Cugat grew up in Cuba and moved to New York when he was a young adult. A gifted musician with a vivid personality, he formed his first band in the twenties, when the tango fad was going strong. When the trend ended, Cugat turned to other types of Latin American music, including the rumba and the mambo. His band played the Miami–New York–Los Angeles circuit and all points in between. Cugat's personality and sense of showmanship appealed to crowds almost as much as his music did. His trademark was the bright red dinner jacket he wore for performances. Between numbers, his snappy patter kept the crowds amused. This proved so popular that Cugat and his orchestra were featured in several films of the era, including *Gay Madrid*, *Weekend at the Waldorf*, and *Bathing Beauty*.

Cugat never felt his showmanship compromised his music, and neither did his audiences. He and his orchestra became the resident group at the Waldorf-Astoria in New York and had regular bookings at Los Angeles's Cocoanut Grove, but he continued to tour cross-country, make movies and records, and appear on the radio well into the sixties. He never missed a chance to introduce the audience to something new and exciting, from the rumba to the mambo to the conga. Clubs that couldn't get Cugat still wanted someone like him, and throughout the thirties and forties every nightclub worth its salt—from the China Doll on the West Coast to the Versailles on the East—offered Latin music and dance for the growing tide of "mambonicks." So ubiquitous was the in-house rumba team that in 1937 a cartoon entitled "Morning, Noon and Night Club" featured the dance team of "Popito" and "Olivita" performing at Wimpy's Cafe while Bluto heckled them from the audience.

June VI, 1943

VICTORY!

THE WAR YEARS

During World War II, people sang, "When the lights go on again all over the world." After initially hurting business, the war soon proved to be the nightclub's best friend. In bars, cabarets, ballrooms, joints, and boîtes all over the world, in London, Cairo, Berlin, and Tokyo, people wanted to escape. Crowding together in noisy clubs to watch a show that had nothing to do with reality turned out to be a surefire remedy for the headlines of the day.

The entertainment business was especially booming in America. Big cities were bursting with people, most of them young, many away from home for the first time, and almost all eager for distraction. There were servicemen in training or waiting to ship out, sisters and girlfriends who had gotten jobs in the surging economy, Red Cross and USO personnel, and engineers, factory workers, and government

employees who continually were transferred and relocated throughout the war. Unemployment, at a level of 9.6 percent in 1940, sank to 1.9 percent by 1943. For the first time in a decade people had money to spend. Shortages prevented splurges on imported and manufactured items; food and gasoline were tightly rationed. But there was no limit on the consumption of entertain-

Last night I accidentally dropped a collar button from my shirt on the floor. An' before I can pick it up a waiter throws a tablecloth right over it an' seats six people.

—JIMMY DURANTE
AT THE COPACABANA, 1943

{ 98 }

CLUB NEW ★ De LISA

4 SHOWS NITELY

VICTORY

AIR CONDITIONED

VICTORY

AIR CONDITIONED

BREAKFAST DANCE EVERY MONDAY MORNING

NO COVER OR MINIMUM CHARGE

ment, and nightclubs jumped to meet the demand. When a midnight curfew was decreed for bars and nightclubs, New York mayor Fiorello La Guardia extended it to 1 A.M., saying servicemen and war workers needed their fun. Although MP's were sent out to enforce the midnight ruling, it was La Guardia who won. The government backed down again when its ill-advised increase of the nightclub tax added to customers' checks, shrank business, and put more than twenty thousand people out of work. After a few months, the tax was cut from 30 percent to its previous 20 percent, and people once again flooded the nighttime pleasure domes.

menu

COCOANUT GROVE

Boston's Cocoanut Grove was one of America's swankiest clubs, a tropical fantasy whose ceiling was draped with miles of indigo satins and whose towering artificial palms trailed green paper fronds tipped with glittering silver. The Club was packed beyond capacity on the night of Saturday, November 28, 1942, when a fire broke out in a downstairs cocktail lounge. Fed by the club's highly combustible décor, flames raced up a narrow stairway and quickly spread throughout the building, exacting a toll of some 500 lives. After the tragedy, fire codes were far more stringently enforced, and nightclub advertising frequently assured patrons that decorations were crafted only of the most up-to-date fireproof materials.

During World War II, clubs recorded their highest returns ever. The Latin Quarter in New York, which initially reported a 25 percent downturn in revenues, was soon packing in crowds every night, as were the Chez Paree in Chicago, the Bal Tarbain in San Francisco, and the Florentine Gardens in Los Angeles. In the ghostly, blacked-out Times Square area, customers waited in long lines to get in. By the end of the war, New York City's nightclubs were grossing more than eighty-five million dollars a year. It wasn't unusual for the Copacabana to average a gross of fifty-five thousand dollars a week; the Latin Quarter, only ten

or fifteen thousand less; and the Zanzibar and Billy Rose's Diamond Horseshoe, a reliable forty thousand dollars each. Ben Marden's Riviera, a splashy palace in New Jersey built along the lines of Rome's Colosseum, claimed to take in over a million dollars a year. Such was the scramble for tables at New York's El Morocco that the headwaiter was said to have made forty thousand dollars a year, almost all of it in tips. It got to the point that Variety joked about head-waiters buying second homes and maître d's retiring to Italy's Lake Como.

In 1944, *Look* magazine estimated that couples were spending a minimum of ten dollars, and usually much more, on an evening out. Not surprisingly, prices in clubs were higher than in ordinary bars. The bottle of beer that cost thirty-five cents at a local tavern cost seventy-five cents at a big-city nightclub. In addition to cover charges, food, and liquor, clubs made money on all manner of souvenirs, from cigarettes to boutonnieres, photographs, dolls, and programs. The high prices did little to discourage customers, though. At every table, between every couple and among every group, nestled the thought that such a night might never be repeated. At such a time, a little economy seemed an enormous waste of possibilities.

THE LAST OF THE RED HOT NIGHTCLUBS

Just as the Stork Club and El Morocco competed to be the best of the "non-nightclub" nightclubs, two other clubs vied to be the showiest of the show clubs. From the forties through the fifties, the Latin Quarter and the Copacabana in New York were the sine qua non of splash and sparkle. Situated on opposite sides of Manhattan, their sprightly revues and large chorus lines reminded customers of the French Casino, the plush club of the thirties whose space was now occupied by Billy Rose's Casa Mañana.

The Latin Quarter

During the nightclub era, it was almost as popular to weave into a club's name the word "Latin" or even "Latin Quarter" as it was to drop in the heady word "Copa." There were several Latin Quarter clubs in America, and in Boston and Chicago they were relatively famous. But *the* Latin Club, like *the* Copa, was located in New York; Times Square. An affiliate branch was later opened in Miami Beach, but Miami Beach wasn't Times Square, and never would be.

Like the earlier French Casino, the Latin Quarter stressed glamour with a European twist. It succeeded on a grand scale, due in large part to the club's stage manager and producer, Lou

Walters. Walters, father of journalist Barbara Walters, wanted revues that incorporated European glamour with American show business. He especially wanted showgirls who were a cut above average, and he regularly traveled to Europe to recruit dancers from Paris and London. As a result, the Latin Quarter's large, twenty-seven-girl chorus line was the most famous in New York. *Life* magazine consistently voted Walters's hand-picked kickline the last word in loveliness, and one of the club's premier dancers, Dale Strong, was named the prettiest showgirl in New York.

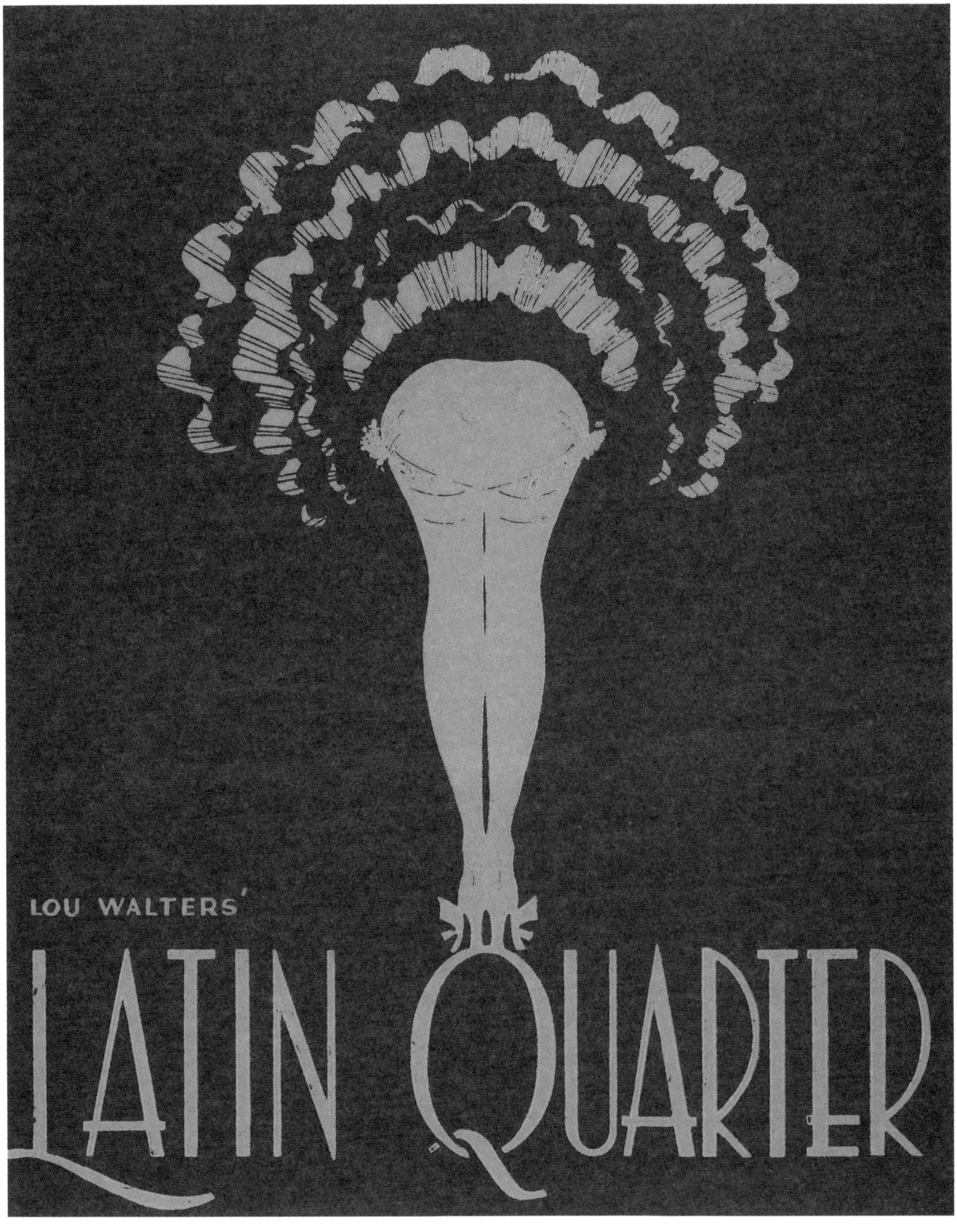
LOU WALTERS'
LATIN QUARTER

A VISIT TO THE
LATIN QUARTER
IS LIKE A TRIP TO PARIS

Continental Charm, joie d'vivre, savoir-faire exemplified in these wonderful cabarets.

Thrilling shows, exquisite girls, stars who come from leading theatres of Europe and America.

In New York on Times Square. In Miami Beach, on Beautiful Palm Island.

In both these thrilling centres of pleasure you see the finest shows, dine in a gracious manner, and are entertained as befits people who insist on the best.

Latin Quarter

Walters made the chorus line one of the club's key drawing cards. Latin Quarter girls became known as the most beautiful, most graceful, and most gorgeously costumed in town; the anonymous but stunning showgirl, shown in pose after pose, became the club's enduring logo. Although the Latin Quarter showgirl never actually appeared nude, club illustrator Wesley Morse promised that she would. His artwork, found in nearly every piece of Latin Quarter memorabilia, illustrated a blend of seductiveness and saucy innocence that bypassed American puritanism in favor of French gaiety.

Like the showgirls, the revues at the Latin Quarter often had a French flavor. There were cancan numbers worthy of the Moulin Rouge, and the club's programs jubilantly proclaimed, "So this is Gay Paree." The magic was that Gay Paree could also become Rio at Mardi Gras or the lobby of the Ritz Hotel. There were two orchestras, Latin and ballroom dance teams, and a generous sprinkling of big-name acts. Jack Benny, Dean Martin and Jerry Lewis, Frank Sinatra, Martha Raye, Sophie Tucker, and Frankie Laine were all regulars at the Latin Quarter. Sitting beneath a ceiling of draped satin and enjoying food and drinks as you were presented with showgirls who descended a row of steps until their high-heeled feet were almost within touching distance—who would have quibbled with the Latin Quarter's claim to being "America's wonder cabaret"?

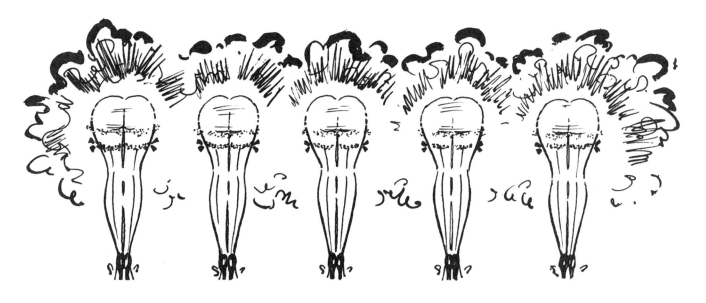

The Copacabana

Across town from the Latin Quarter was the Copacabana. Located just off Fifth Avenue on East Sixtieth Street, the Copa wasn't the most profitable nightclub, but it was by far the biggest and most famous showplace of the era. Entertainers considered it the mecca of the nightclub world—the Carnegie Hall of nightclubs—a sure sign that one had reached the pinnacle of fame.

The club got its start in 1940, when the former Villa Valle restaurant in the Hotel Four-teen closed and Monte Proser and Jules Podell leased the twelve-thousand-square-foot space for one hundred thousand dollars a year. Persistent rumors also named a silent partner, Frank Costello (of Saratoga gambling fame and head of one of New York's mafia families), but the club itself was "clean." There was no illegal gambling allowed, and the club never had a record of tax or ordinance violations.

You're a show business nobody until you make the Copa and do three shows nightly under its tremendous pastel roof.

—FRANK SINATRA

Named for the famous Rio de Janeiro resort, the Copacabana had a Brazilian flavor that appealed to the craze for Latin music and culture. The club's logo was a sultry beauty with a pouty mouth and a striped turban spilling grapes and bananas. Many people believed the logo—by Wesley Morse, also the Latin Quarter's illustrator—represented South American actress Carmen Miranda. In fact, it's probable that the model for the piece was the wife of entertainer Jan Murray. Whoever the model was, the headdress became famous in its own right. The "Copa bonnet," as it was called, served as the club's very own Academy Award, given to the biggest of the big-name acts. Frank Sinatra, Lena Horne, Vic Damone, Jimmy Durante, Danny Thomas, and Dean Martin and Jerry Lewis all were proud recipients of the coveted bonnet.

COPACABANA
NEW YORK

MINIMUM CHARGE

Eight Dollars Fifty Cents Nightly
Nine Dollars Fifty Cents Saturdays
(Per Person)

The minimum may be consumed in
food, beverages, or both.

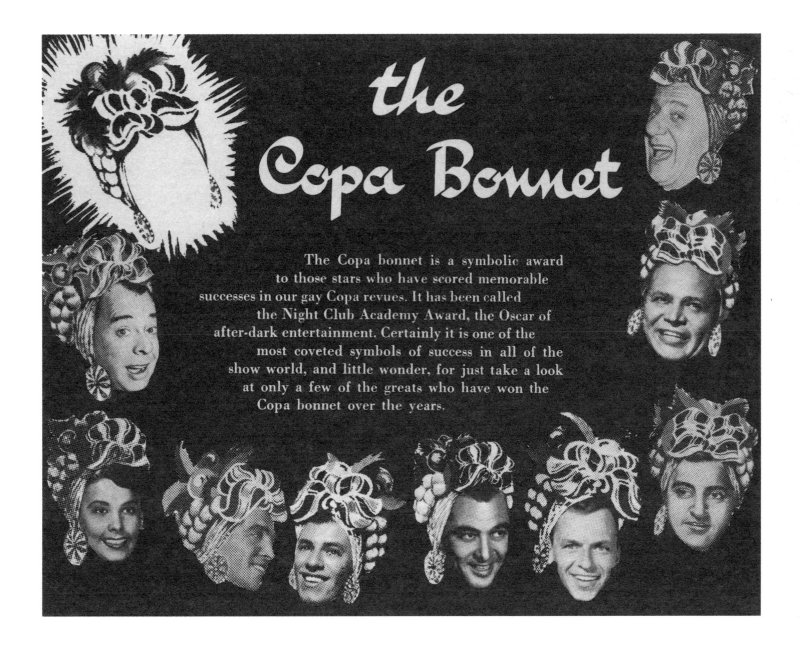

the Copa Bonnet

The Copa bonnet is a symbolic award to those stars who have scored memorable successes in our gay Copa revues. It has been called the Night Club Academy Award, the Oscar of after-dark entertainment. Certainly it is one of the most coveted symbols of success in all of the show world, and little wonder, for just take a look at only a few of the greats who have won the Copa bonnet over the years.

At least as alluring as the Copa's headliners were its showgirls. Always in competition with the Latin Quarter in the sequins-and-spangles department, the Copa mounted a ritzy chorus line. Showgirls' upswept coifs were often dyed pink, green, or gold to match their outfits; the costumes for each dancer—including not only turbans festooned with fruit but mink panties and bras—were calculated at the end of the forties to cost in excess of four thousand dollars per girl.

LOSS OF THE VOICE

© Bettman/Corbis

Frank Sinatra rode the success elevator close to the top by 1950, but he was still working three shows a night at the Copa and pursuing a full-time recording career. He recorded over two dozen singles for Columbia in 1949 and another fifteen in the first four months of 1950. On April 24, he had just finished a four-record session adding "When You're Smiling," "It's Only a Paper Moon," "My Blue Heaven," and "The Continental" to his discography. Two days later, he took the stage as usual for the third show at the Copa.

The weather was bad that Wednesday evening, and there were less than a hundred patrons in the club's enormous showroom. When Sinatra stepped up to the microphone and started to sing, nothing came out. "I was never so panicked in my life," he said later. "There was absolute silence—stunning, absolute silence." Skitch Henderson, who was conducting the orchestra that night, saw the panic. Sinatra's face turned chalk white and, after managing a rasping "good night," he left the stage. The audience, aware that something was wrong, sat in shocked silence.

A doctor's examination proved how serious the incident was. After weeks of overwork and stress, Sinatra's vocal chords had ruptured. For the next forty days, he was forbidden to utter a sound, and it was uncertain whether or not his voice ever again would be the same. The episode marked the first setback in a career that was characterized by an uncommon number of highs and lows. Sinatra resumed singing within a few months, but his voice as well as his self-confidence were shaken. He was despondent and feared that, at age thirty-five, his career was over. It was not until he portrayed Maggio in 1953's *From Here to Eternity* that Sinatra found his career footing and once again became "The Voice."

TRÈS CIRQUE!

REVUE

FLORENTINE
Gardens

The Florentine Gardens

If World War II created a boom on America's East Coast and heartland, it caused an even greater boom in the West. Naval bases, shipyards, and aircraft factories from San Diego to Puget Sound prompted a wave of migration, drawing people from all over the country. Between 1940 and 1944, the population of San Diego County increased by 44 percent, the San Francisco Bay Area by 25 percent, and the Los Angeles region by 15 percent. Many of the newcomers would go home after the war, but while they were there they were eager for a good time.

In San Francisco they flocked to the Bal Tarbain, the Club Lido, and the festive Monaco, the latter of which catered to families and, in a bow to the home of the future Princess Grace, served up a dish called "Chicken à la Grimaldi." There were the Chinatown clubs and Finocchio's, famous for its female impersonators. In Los Angeles there was the lush Cocoanut Grove in the Ambassador Hotel, Earl Carroll's cavernous Theatre-Restaurant, and Slapsy Maxie's, run by former prize fighter Slapsy Maxie Rosenbloom. At Ciro's, proprietor Herman Hover bought his booze directly from Joe Kennedy and could get aged Scotch when no one else could. (No wonder Ciro's was the favorite haunt of Frank Sinatra and Howard Hughes.)

By far the splashiest club of the war era was the Florentine Gardens, located in the glitzy district of Hollywood Boulevard. The club's producer was Nils Thor Granlund, a sort of Swedish-born Billy Rose. Like Rose, Granlund—known more commonly as N.T.G.—had a

flair for publicity and promotion. He invented the movie premiere, with its flock of celebrities, floodlights, and heavy press coverage. In New York he ran the Hollywood Restaurant, one of the first places to combine food with a floor show.

The Gardens opened under Granlund's directorship in the spring of 1940. From its curving neon-and-deco piedmont and scallop-shell awning to its circular, one-thousand-seat showroom, the place seemed determined to offer up the best—or at least the most—in the way of over-the-top entertainment. It became so famous for this that in 1944 *Life* magazine asserted that the club was too well-known to draw movie celebrities, who felt more at ease in the "exclusive intimacy" of the Macombo, the Clover Club, and the Trocadero. The non-celebrities didn't seem to mind the club's fame a bit. They were there to see the show and dance to Paul Whiteman's orchestra. Throughout the war, Granlund's club was sold-out almost every night of the week. Spillover customers could decamp to the club's new, grass-thatched ZanziBar lounge, where the Mills Brothers frequently sang and the artist-in-residence was a lei-bedecked hula dancer.

Like the Latin Quarter and the Copacabana, the Florentine Gardens mixed headline acts with extravagantly costumed showgirls in loosely themed production numbers. During the war, one revue entitled "Red, White, and Beautiful" featured a number called "What We Do Without" in which various showgirls appeared as Tires, Sugar, Silk, and Paper. In case the revue itself didn't hold customers' attention, Granlund also incorporated several circus acts. At some point during the evening, five beautiful girls would dangle from the ceiling on ropes and Elly Ardelty, "the Venus of the air," would sail across the room on her golden trapeze.

The Florentine Gardens scene was a little raucous, but just what the bromide the doctor ordered to soothe away the jitters of war.

THE LAST TIME I SAW PARIS

The Moulin Rouge

The world that existed after World War II was not the same world that had rushed off to war six years earlier. Much of Europe lay in ruin—destroyed, impoverished, occupied, or a combination of all three. New fissures had developed, separating East from West and closing millions behind an iron curtain. Even in America, which enjoyed an enormous postwar economic boom, returning soldiers and the women who waited for them discovered a simple fact: it was *good* to be home. People married, had children, and moved to the suburbs in record numbers—a nationwide nesting orgy that had a lethal effect on nightlife. Couples who previously could hop in a cab to get to a nightclub now found they had to hire a baby-sitter and drive into the city. Why go to the trouble when you could stay home and watch *The Milton Berle Show* on your new television set?

Few new nightclubs emerged during the fifties, but one worth noting is Frank Sennes's Moulin Rouge in Hollywood. A West Coast showman, Sennes had a fine eye for talent and previously had been the producer at the Hollywood Gardens nightclub. He gave the unknown Betty Grable a job as a showgirl, and was among the first to book singers Frankie Laine and Perry Como, who earned three dollars a night and thirty-five dollars a week respectively.

After Earl Carroll's death in 1948, his Theatre-Restaurant was vacant. Despite warnings from friends and colleagues that the days of the big, lavish nightclub were waning, Sennes wanted to refurbish the space in the tradition of the French Casino and other grand old Parisienne-themed clubs of the past.

FRANK SENNES with FERNANDO LAMAS and ARLENE DAHL

RITA MORENO

BOB HOPE,
JIMMIE DURANTE,
MILTON BERLE,
and
DANNY THOMAS

ESTHER WILLIAMS and BEN GAGE

RHONDA
FLEMMING

LUCILLE BALL and
GORDON MacRAE

NOEL COWARD and JEAN SIMMONS

ROSEMARY BOWE and
ROBERT STACK

The Moulin Rouge opened in Carroll's former space in the early fifties, with revues as splashy as anything ever seen. True to its French theme, revues had titles like "Voici! Paris!," "Ça C'est Paris!," and "Paris Toujours." There were Folies–style as well as Latin numbers, and carnival acts that involved two rings and a fleet of acrobats and aerialists and at least one trained elephant. There were headliners like Jimmy Durante, singer Johnny Ray, and comic bandleader Spike Jones. There was everything a nightclub could offer, including special Sunday matinees that catered to all those newly formed, suburban-dwelling families. To help pay the rent on the place, Sennes also leased the space for trade shows and special events. For several years, the Moulin Rouge delivered all the glitter and glamour anyone could want; but it was glamour and glitter from a rapidly vanishing world. By the end of the fifties it was clear that the era of the big club really was over. The Moulin Rouge closed. The building, which had housed the spectacular productions of Frank Sennes as well as Earl Carroll before him, eventually became the Aquarius Theater, where, appropriately, the musical *Hair!* played in the sixties.

the Painted Desert Room

AMERICA'S SMARTEST SUPPER CLUB . . . . .

Presents . . . .

THAT LITTLE SPOT IN THE DESERT

Las Vegas

As anyone who has seen *The Godfather*—or the host of wise-guy movies that followed it—knows, Las Vegas was nothing until Bugsy Siegel and his friends got ahold of it. The truth, left on the cutting room floor, is a bit stickier than that. The famous Las Vegas Strip really began in 1938 when a California hotelier named Tomas Hull decided that a resort with a highly visible, invitingly cool swimming pool was just the thing to lure motorists off the highway. Hull's El Rancho resort and casino opened in 1941 and soon proved him right. Because the scenery wasn't much to look at and there was no place else to go, El Rancho added food and entertainment. It was tinsel without the town, and Hollywood celebrities discovered they could relax and mingle without the usual horde of star-hungry autograph seekers. When word leaked out that the place was becoming a celebrity magnet, ordinary folks started coming, too. To accommodate the rush, a few more resorts and casinos had to be built. Next came a place called The Last Frontier and then, in 1946, Bugsy Seigel's visionary Flamingo.

Siegel and his partners wanted more than a scattering of hotels on the outskirts of Vegas. They literally wanted to recreate the glamour of Hollywood's Sunset Strip.

MUSIC FOR SHOW AND DANCING BY
CARLTON HAYES & ORCHESTRA

Their plans were so ambitious that they had to hold a grand opening before the place was finished in order to raise the money to complete it. The "opening" was a debacle—rooms weren't finished and many Hollywood guests were kept in Los Angeles by bad weather. The show, however, was a success—Jimmy Durante delivered his usual dynamite performance and ended the show by demolishing a piano and scattering Xavier Cugat's sheet music around the room.

Soon the Sands opened and gave the show in the Flamingo a run for its money. Both resorts spent huge amounts of money to bring in big-name acts, and both succeeded. Jimmy Durante, Pearl Bailey, Lena Horne, Tony Martin, Dean Martin and Jerry Lewis, Shelley Winters, Kay Starr, the Ink Spots, Brenda Lee, Kaye Ballard, Ted Lewis, Noel Coward—*everybody* played Vegas. Even Judy Garland played the Flamingo in 1957, taking the opportunity to introduce her eleven-year-old daughter, Liza Minnelli, on stage.

For a time, it seemed as if Las Vegas might be the nightclub's salvation, a place where the Copacabanas and Latin Quarters of the world could continue just as they always had. Even the names were reminiscent of the boom clubs of the thirties and

forties—the Tropicana, the Casino de Paris, the Silver Slipper, the Trocadero. When the Sands Hotel opened in 1952, it seemed a thrilling assurance that the nightclub era would continue forever.

To those who felt a bit disoriented by the carefully watered palm trees, clattering dice, and looping azure swimming pools, the Sands offered a bit of home. One of the partners was Jack Entratter, a veteran of New York's Stork Club and Copacabana. A favorite of performers, Entratter successfully lured the biggest of the big-name acts away from the Flamingo and the Desert Inn. To make these stars feel especially at home, he christened the showroom the Copa Room, dubbed the chorus line the Copa Girls, and made sure there was plenty of Chinese food in the house. Because the Sands was the only club that allowed patrons to get to their rooms without passing through the casino, guests could almost forget they were in Las Vegas. During its first six months of operation, from mid-December of 1952 to mid-June of 1953, Danny Thomas, Frank Sinatra, Dean Martin and Jerry Lewis, Lena Horne, Tony Bennett, Nat King Cole, Red Skelton, and Milton Berle all played the Copa Room. Frank Sinatra especially made Entratter's new club his home, and it was here that the Rat Pack—made up of Sinatra, Dean Martin, Peter Lawford, Sammy Davis, Jr., and Joey Bishop—played regularly for years.

Years later, Sinatra got into a scuffle with the club's casino manager, and the Rat Pack moved to Caesar's Palace. By then, though, it was clear that Las Vegas wasn't the nightclub scene of old and never would be. The problem was that there was simply

We haven't seen much daylight since we've been here.

Seen a lot of Jack Daniels, but not much daylight.

—FRANK SINATRA, AT THE SANDS'S COPA ROOM

too much of everything. In the golden days of the nightclub era, each club was a unique fantasy, a big bubble of a world floating brightly above the gritty reality of traffic and the dark, chilly streets outside. In Las Vegas, the fantasy was so big it swallowed up all those bubbles. The whole Las Vegas Strip was a nonstop fantasy, a glitzy, fifty-ring circus. What had seemed impossibly wonderful in New York or Miami just seemed commonplace in Las Vegas.

In the end, Las Vegas became an entity completely its own, a world of high stakes and high hopes, where "floating crap game" wasn't just a figure of speech but an actual raft in the shallow end of the pool, frequented by celebrities standing in waist-deep water. Today Vegas has once again reinvented itself, this time as a playland pieced together from block-long strips of other countries. The latest nostalgia isn't for the nightclubs of World War II but for the original Vegas—the lounge-and-cigarette-smoke Vegas, the ring-a-ding-ding Vegas of Sinatra and the Rat Pack. The nightclub-era ghosts one could sometimes glimpse in that Vegas have disappeared, crushed beneath the weight of the new new thing. Now and then the lost world shines forth in the midnight sparkle of sequin, but only rarely, when the moon and memories are just right.

ILLUSTRATIONS

SELECT BIBLIOGRAPHY

Blumenthal, Ralph. *Stork Club*. New York: Little Brown, 2000.

DeMatteo, Deanna. Las Vegas Strip Historical Sight; http://www.lvstriphistory.com

"Florentine Gardens." *Life*, January 31, 1944.

Gavin, James. *Intimate Nights: The Golden Age of New York Cabaret*. New York: Grove Weidenfeld, 1991.

Gottlieb, Polly Rose. *The Nine Lives of Billy Rose*. New York: Crown Publishers, 1968.

Green, Abel and Joe Laurie, Jr. *Show Biz From Vaude to Video*. New York: Henry Holt, 1951.

Haskins, Jim. *The Cotton Club*. New York: Random House, 1977.

Jones, Jay. *Billy Rose Presents . . . Casa Mañana*. Fort Worth: TCU Press, 1999.

Keyes, Edward. *Cocoanut Grove*. New York: Atheneum, 1984.

Lahr, John. *Sinatra*. New York: Random House, 1997.

Levy, Shawn. *Rat Pack Confidential*. New York: Doubleday, 1998.

Lingeman, Richard. *Don't You Know There's a War On?* New York: Putnam, 1970.

"Manhattan Night Life." *Fortune*, March, 1936.

Margolick, David. *Strange Fruit: Billie Holiday, Cafe Society, and an Early Cry for Civil Rights*. Philadelphia: Running Press, 2000.

Mosedale, John. *The Men Who Invented Broadway: Damon Runyan, Walter Winchell & Their World*. New York: Richard Marek Publishers, 1981.

Murray, Ken. *The Body Merchant: The Story of Earl Carroll*. Pasadena: Ward Ritchie Press, 1976.

"Night Clubs: They Are Enjoying the Greatest Boom in Their History." *Look,* 1944.

Reich, Howard. "Viva Las Vegas: Old-Fashioned Glitz and Glamour Live on at Havana's Fabulous Tropicana." *Chicago Tribune*, January 14, 1999.

Robbins, Jhan. *Inka Dinka Doo: The Life of Jimmy Durante*. New York: Paragon House, 1991.

Rosenblum, Constance. *Gold Digger: The Outrageous Life and Times of Peggy Hopkins Joyce*. New York: Metropolitan Books/Henry Holt, 2000.

Tosches, Nick. *Dino: Living High in the Dirty Business of Dreams*. New York: Doubleday, 1992.

Walker, Stanley. *The Night Club Era*. New York: Blue Ribbon Books, 1933.

Zehme, Bill. *The Way You Wear Your Hat: Frank Sinatra and the Lost Art of Livin'*. New York: Harper Collins, 1997.

Susan Waggoner is a writer of nonfiction and fiction books, including
Vintage Cocktails: Authentic Recipes and Illustrations from 1920-1960 and
The Women's Sports Encyclopedia. A native of Minnesota and an alumni of
the Iowa Writer's Workshop, she currently lives in New York City.